The 5 BigLies About American Business

Combating Smears
Against the Free-Market Economy

Michael Medved

CROWN
FORUM
NEW YORK

All rights reserved.
Published in the United States by Crown Forum,
an imprint of the Crown Publishing Group, a division
of Random House, Inc., New York.
www.crownpublishing.com

CROWN FORUM with colophon is a registered trademark
of Random House, Inc.

Grateful acknowledgment is made to the following for the photos and illustrations
in this book:

p. 32: Illustration courtesy of Art Young; *p. 61: From the Depths* by Wm. Balfour-Ker.
(1905), courtesy of Prints & Photographs Division, Library of Congress; *p. 100:*
Illustration by Walt McDougall, *New York World,* 1884; *p. 141:* Photo courtesy of the
Library of Congress, Prints & Photographs Division, FSA/OWI Collection; *p. 182:* Photo
courtesy of the George Grantham Bain Collection, Prints & Photographs Division,
Library of Congress.

Library of Congress Cataloging-in-Publication Data is available upon request.

ISBN 978-0-307-46494-1

Printed in the United States of America

Design based on a design by Lauren Dong

10 9 8 7 6 5 4 3 2 1

First Edition

For my parents
David Bernard Medved (1926–2009)
Renate Hirsch Medved (1924–2000)
They taught us to value creativity—and business

CONTENTS

Industry gives comfort and plenty and respect.

—BENJAMIN FRANKLIN

After all, the chief business of the American people is business. They are profoundly concerned with producing, buying, selling, investing and prospering in the world. I am strongly of the opinion that the great majority of people will always find these are moving impulses of our life.

—CALVIN COOLIDGE

Business was originated to produce happiness.

—BERTIE CHARLES FORBES

Embarrassed by Business

Dr. David Medved, "scientist and entrepreneur," 1964

THE UNACKNOWLEDGED ENTREPRENEUR

When my father died in March 2009, I felt startled by obituaries that identified him as a "scientist *and entrepreneur.*"

A scientist . . . well, of course, but at no point in my life had it occurred to me to describe my dad as an "entrepreneur" or "businessman." When speaking about him, I always proudly announced his profession as "physicist," or "physics professor," or "NASA researcher," or even as "scientist astronaut." (He qualified for the Apollo Program in the late 1960s but never received his final mission assignment from NASA because of some minor problems with his teeth and gums.) At one point during my senior year at Yale, I jokingly introduced my father to my friends as "a member of the military-industrial complex"—a designation my dad always remembered and savored. As an aspiring intellectual, with dreams of future glory in writing or politics, I could handle the idea that my brilliant, adventurous papa played a role in the defense establishment, but I couldn't accept the notion that he qualified as an ordinary, moneygrubbing capitalist. Stressing his government or academic work provided a much better way to impress my pals, or the women I pursued, or even complete strangers, but I've come to realize that this emphasis seriously distorted the focus of his work life.

During the weeklong mourning period for my father, I sat with my brothers in Jerusalem (where my dad chose to spend his final two decades) and we jointly reviewed the way he had invested his eighty-three years. He spent less than nine years as a university professor (part-time at San Diego State and then, briefly, full-time at UCLA), and just five years as an experimenter and prospective astronaut with NASA. He devoted more than forty years, however, to an all-consuming career as an entrepreneur and creator of high-tech companies, building two moderately successful businesses from scratch. First came MERET Inc. (founded in the family den in West L.A., the name stood for Medved Research and Technology), and then JOLT in Jerusalem (another nifty acronym—Jerusalem Optical Link Technology). He toiled lovingly, tirelessly, and joyously on both ventures, providing jobs for scores of bright, eager, mostly younger associates (including my brother Jonathan), before selling each enterprise to much larger, more established firms. Even after he gave up ownership and day-to-day command of JOLT, he retained a position as the firm's "chief scientist" and continued to busy himself with every aspect of the corporation's scientific and commercial affairs. He worked full-time for the company he created until just days before his brief, final hospitalization with recurrent lymphoma.

On the long flight back from Israel, while sorting through a large file of old family letters and clippings from my dad's apartment, I suddenly confronted another uncomfortable realization: it wasn't just my father who had invested most of his energy and ambition in the world of business. By any honest accounting, I'd always earned my own living in some form of corporate, for-profit enterprise as well—either the book business, the radio-TV business, the movie business, the newspaper business, or (for a few years after law school) the political consulting business. My three brothers owed their livelihoods to fiercely competitive commercial careers even more directly—one of them as a well-known venture capitalist and entrepreneur in Israel, another as a marriage and family therapist managing an independent practice in Silicon Valley, and the youngest as a respected executive for the California-based movie-ticketing company Fandango.

Our extended family boasted an even broader, deeper involvement in building businesses. Going back to the immigrant generation, it's true that my father's father toiled with his hands as a salaried barrel maker, but my other grandfather, my mother's father, spent his whole life running small, successful pudding and chocolate companies—first in Germany and later in Philadelphia. His son, my Uncle Fritz, moved with grace and humor through a variety of business positions, including a cherished stint running a popular deli in downtown Philly. Meanwhile, my Uncle Moish, my dad's only brother, became a local legend with his Jewish community activism and his forty years as proprietor and principal of a home electrical service; he decorated his two bright-blue panel trucks with the biblical slogan "Let There Be Light!"

Given this colorful and scrappy background in American commerce, why did my brothers and I share such an awkward reluctance to describe ourselves as a business family, preferring on most occasions to associate ourselves with intellectual, media, or political pursuits? When we owed everything—*everything*—to the free-market system, why did we feel occasionally embarrassed by our family's business ties, treating the realm of profit-seeking enterprise as a necessary evil rather than a glory of civilization?

Like many other children in countless families across the country, we unresistingly imbibed the antibusiness bias that's pervaded American culture since the Great Depression. We got the message that corporations crushed sensitivity and decency, promoting ruthless manipulation with their crude emphasis on the bottom line, but we never probed too deeply into how, exactly, our parents provided for the pleasant circumstances of our lives. In retrospect, it's amazing that neither my dad nor my uncles nor any of the business-oriented friends of the family ever bothered to correct our puerile assumptions about the corruptions of capitalism. Perhaps they dismissed some of the prevailing ideas as too stupid, too shallow and immature, to merit serious challenge and assumed we would eventually outgrow them as we accumulated practical experience.

As a result, I grew up, like most of my fellow baby boomers (not to mention the offspring of later generations), with an in-

stinctive acceptance of a series of big lies about American business. This book means to answer those distortions with the sort
of rebuttals seldom encountered in schools, pop culture, or
news media. The economic crisis that shook the country in
2008–2009 makes these responses all the more urgent. The financial reverses afflicting the United States (and all other major
economies) encourage the public to believe the worst about our
business system and even to expect its imminent demise.

DISMISSING AND DISTRUSTING
THE PROFIT MOTIVE

While hard times unquestionably intensify popular suspicions
about the values and practices of corporate America, the widespread skepticism toward the market economy began long before the current downturn. Ever since FDR's New Deal of the
1930s, and perhaps since the Progressive Era of thirty years before, the public has expressed queasiness and uncertainty regarding the profit motive. In most quarters of our society there's
no shame in possessing money (or the flashy signifiers of wealth
and luxury) but there is an odd discomfort in admitting the
means by which those resources were acquired. We all benefit
from the unparalleled and prodigious productivity of the capitalist system but we feel reluctant to accept the vigorous pursuit
of profit at its very core.

Recent surveys, for instance, display startling levels of contempt for leaders of business, reflecting the assumption that entrepreneurs and executives count as sleazy, greedy, selfish, and
unreliable. In February 2009, a Harris Interactive poll asked
1,050 respondents if "people on Wall Street" were "as honest

and moral as other people"; a stunning 70 percent said "no." In November 2008, an annual Gallup poll evaluated the "Honesty and Ethics of Professions." The category "business executives" ranked near the bottom, even below such frequently reviled occupations as "Lawyers," "Labor Union Leaders," "Funeral Directors," and "Real Estate Agents." (The businessmen beat out only "Congressmen," "Car Salesmen," "Telemarketers," "Advertising Practitioners," and, at the very bottom of the barrel, "Lobbyists.")

In a similar survey of "America's Most Admired Professions" for the Harris organization, the designation "Business Executive" fared even worse. The bulk of 1,020 respondents felt that these capitalist commanders deserved "hardly any prestige at all," ranking them 21st out of 23 categories—barely outpolling only "Stock Broker" and "Real Estate Agent." The most prestigious professions, in order, were "Firefighter," "Doctor," "Nurse," "Scientist," "Teacher," "Military Officer," "Police Officer," "Clergyman," "Farmer," and "Engineer." As *Forbes* magazine aptly observed, "None of top-ten most admired jobs can be accurately described as being driven by the profit motive—quite a contradiction in a country that was built on it. The A-list is comprised of those who serve others, including engineers (they build things) and farmers (who 'feed the world')."

Surprisingly, this survey appeared in the summer of 2006, well before the financial meltdown of September 2008 provoked a fresh tidal wave of stories about corporate malfeasance and the collapse of capitalism. For a major segment of the public and, perhaps, for a majority, attitudes toward the business community have remained overwhelmingly negative, regardless of the ups and downs of the stock market or the unemployment rate. Most frequently, this antagonism begins in childhood, with school curricula that downplay the prominent participation of corporations, free enterprise, and the accumulation of wealth in the development of the United States.

CENSORING AND SLANTING
THE AMERICAN STORY

Even the most cursory examination of elementary and middle school textbooks reveals the present tendency to distort or ignore the role of business in building the country. Consider the national holidays celebrated in the course of an academic year.

- For Thanksgiving, kids learn all about the idealistic Pilgrims and their interaction with the Indians, but hear nothing about their obsessive concern to make their colony profitable or their sponsorship by a for-profit corporation back in England, the London Company.

- Elementary school students prepare for Presidents' Day by studying Lincoln, the Great Emancipator, and Washington, the military hero and Father of Our Country, but they spend no time acknowledging the deep business involvements of both men. Lincoln became prosperous and prominent (by the provincial standards of Springfield, Illinois) by pursuing a career as a corporate lawyer, specializing in representing railroads and other dynamic enterprises. Washington, meanwhile, became one of the richest plantation owners in the colonies through his land investments and the canny management of the resources he acquired after marriage to the wealthy widow Martha. In contrast to his careless Virginia colleague, Thomas Jefferson, he cared deeply about his financial status and avoided debt and money-losing ventures.

- In anticipation of the fireworks of the Fourth of July, most kids get some exposure to the revolutionary slogan "No taxation without representation," but they never connect it to the fact that nearly all our Founders were entrepreneurial merchants and farmers ready to risk their lives to prevent undue governmental interference in their business affairs.

- Finally, we focus on the nation's military history on Memorial Day and Veterans Day, but we seldom acknowledge that the country's greatest military victories owe as much to our economic power and prosperity as to our soldiers' battlefield courage. The Union forces prevailed in the War Between the States because the industrial might of the North easily outproduced the Confederacy. In World War I, America rescued our struggling British and French allies as much with financial support as with a massive expeditionary force, and twenty-seven years later the unprecedented manufacture of planes, warships, tanks, landing craft, and, ultimately, atom bombs played an utterly decisive part in crushing the Germans and the Japanese. In the forty-five-year struggle against Communism in the Cold War, Americans shed blood in Korea, Vietnam, and elsewhere, but finally prevailed because of the vastly superior productivity and prosperity of our economic system.

When social studies classes review stories about American heroes, they naturally feature inspiring tales about the civil rights activism of Martin Luther King, of the pioneering feminism of suffragists like Susan B. Anthony, or the fierce resistance of Indian warriors like Tecumseh or Sitting Bull. Students may even learn of the amazing contributions of "inventor" Thomas Edison, but they'll hear nothing about the time and energy he invested in building major corporations to make sure he enjoyed the monetary rewards of his technological breakthroughs, and vanquished his competitors. Despite media fascination with the current corporate titans like Donald Trump and Bill Gates, no business leader of the past occupies a place on the A-list in the American pantheon. If youngsters hear anything at all about the builders and bosses (Rockefeller, Carnegie, Ford, and many more) who made the nation the world's dominant power, they are most likely to concentrate on sneering accounts of their exploitations and predations as "robber barons."

"A TIME BOMB UNDER AMERICAN CAPITALISM"

Literature classes also contribute to the prevailing cynicism about industrialists, entrepreneurs, and financiers; the further students progress in their educations, the greater the chance that they'll learn contempt for business. At the most basic level, commercial success in a market economy stems from the simple expedient of selling a product or service for more than it costs to provide it, just as the steady accumulation of wealth requires nothing more than keeping your expenditures somewhere below your income. These practical imperatives inevitably conflict with the unfocused flightiness of adolescence, so that adolescents (of all ages) contend that the endless repetition of such hardheaded transactions will necessarily deaden the spirit and paralyze the imagination. As young people occupy bedrooms at home or bunk comfortably at college dorms, enjoying the worthy pursuit of educational progress (and weekend partying) financed by their parents' generosity, it's easy to embrace the romantic spirit of the cherished 1806 lyric by William Wordsworth:

> *The world is too much with us; late and soon,*
> *Getting and spending, we lay waste our powers:*

A defender of the market system might point out that the orderly and disciplined process of "getting and spending" is more likely to enhance rather than "lay waste" our powers, but the characterization of business toil as a desensitizing, soul-killing process has kept its hold on artists and intellectuals for more than two centuries.

Unfortunately, most Americans encounter the classics in their English classes several years prior to racking up any meaningful firsthand experience in the world of work, so they're conditioned to expect the worst from the business system before they even enter it. Few citizens will escape from the educational system without encountering Arthur Miller's tragic victim of the American dream, the downtrodden plugger Willy Loman (Low-Man, get it?) from his 1949 classic, *Death of a Salesman*. In the "Student Companion to Arthur Miller," Susan C. W. Abbotson writes, "Since his college days, Miller had felt that America was being run by men of business who were all after private profit, and who merely used those without wealth as pawns.

Thus, it made sense to see money and finance as being behind many American conflicts. Howard Wagner, in 'Death of a Salesman', is the epitome of the cold-hearted businessman, who callously takes away Willy Loman's job when he starts to lose business, without a thought to the man's financial obligations and years of service."

Contemplating the value of his life insurance to his family in Act Two, Willy himself declares, "After all the highways, and the trains, and the appointments, and the years, you end up worth more dead than alive." On opening night for the play, a woman called *Death of a Salesman* a "time bomb under American capitalism," and Miller responded that he hoped that it was, or "at least under the bulls—t of capitalism, this pseudo life that thought to touch the clouds by standing on top of a refrigerator, waving a paid-up mortgage at the moon, victorious at last."

Even before Arthur Miller won riches and praise (and Marilyn Monroe) for his indictment of the values of the American market system, literary lions of the 1920s ferociously flayed the "go-getter" business boosters of their era. Sinclair Lewis became the first American to win the Nobel Prize for Literature for a specific citation for his contribution in writing *Babbitt* (1922)— a savage bestselling portrayal of a smug midwestern businessman using "pep" and "pow" to cover the appalling emptiness of their money-obsessed, uncompromisingly conventional middle-class lives. Editor and culture critic H. L. Mencken simultaneously assaulted the same business caste as "the Booboisie," defined by him as "a class of people composed of the stupid and the gullible."

This contempt for the commercial values among the artistic and journalistic elite long preceded the painful dislocations and disillusionments of the Stock Market Crash and the Great Depression. By the time Franklin Roosevelt took over the White House for the first of his four elected terms, the hostility and scorn for captains of capitalism had migrated from the magazines and salons of supercilious mandarins, and from the sweaty Grange or union halls of rural or urban radicals, into the mainstream of the nation's politics and pop culture. Before the Depression, antagonism to the dynamic, explosively expanding commercial system came from those conspicuously left behind—particularly embattled agrarians with failing farms, or unskilled laborers who worked at or below subsistence wages. By 1933, however, most of the country felt left behind or left out with regard to the country's long-prevailing prosperity, and in his celebrated inaugural address, Roosevelt spoke accordingly.

In the course of his most famous speech, FDR not only warned about the paralyzing impact of "fear itself" but also denounced "the rulers of the exchange of mankind's goods" in harsh and sweeping terms that would have been unthinkable for a president of an earlier era. "Practices of the unscrupulous money changers stand indicted in the court of public opinion, rejected by the hearts and minds of men," thundered the new chief executive, in unmistakably biblical terms. "Stripped of the lure of profit by which to induce our people to follow their false leadership, they have resorted to exhortations, pleading tearfully for restored conditions. They know only the rules of a generation of self-seekers.

"They have no vision, and when there is no vision the people perish.

"The money changers have fled their high seats in the temple of our civilization. We may now restore that temple to the ancient truths.

"THE CHIEF BUSINESS OF THE AMERICAN PEOPLE IS . . . IDEALISM"?

How can major media outlets portray business accurately and impartially if they themselves function as major businesses? This conundrum drew memorable comment from President Calvin Coolidge in a stunningly substantive speech to the American Society of Newspaper Editors in 1925. The most infamous Coolidge quote—"The business of America is business"—is actually a wildly distorted and out-of-context version of a passage in this thoughtful address:

> There does not seem to be cause for alarm in the dual relationship of the press to the public, whereby it is on one side a purveyor of information and opinion and on the other side a purely business enterprise. Rather, it is probable that a press which maintains an intimate touch with the business currents of the nation is likely to be more reliable than it would be if it were a stranger to these influences. After all, the chief business of the American people is business. They are profoundly concerned with producing, buying, selling, inventing and prospering in the world. I am strongly of the opinion that the great majority of people will always find these are moving impulses of our life.

Meanwhile, the president went to great lengths to make clear to the editors that they would fail if they ever assumed that even these important "moving impulses of our life" utterly dominated national priorities. "It is only those who do not understand our people, who believe that our national life is entirely absorbed by material motives," he declared near the conclusion of his address. "We make no concealment of the fact that we want wealth, but there are many other things that we want very much more. We want peace and honor, and that charity which is so strong an element of all civilization. The chief ideal of the American people is ideal-ism. I cannot repeat too often that America is a nation of ide-alists. That is the only motive to which they ever give any strong and lasting reaction. No newspaper can be a success which fails to appeal to that element of our national life."

"The measure of the restoration lies in the extent to which we apply social values more noble than mere monetary profit."

Amazingly, at a moment of acute financial crisis and uncer-tainty in the business community, Roosevelt sought to return confidence and vitality to the free-market system by denounc-ing (repeatedly) the pursuit of profit. In his stirring speech, he presented no specific cures for the devastation of the Depres-sion but he affixed unequivocal and exclusive blame for the na-tional catastrophe on the "unscrupulous money changers."

"THE CHILDREN OF GORDON GEKKO"

Growing up in a family that worshipped Roosevelt (my im-migrant grandmother kept a framed photo of the late presi-dent on her living room wall till the day of her death in 1961), I saw no reason to question FDR's indictment of the "economic royalists"—that capitalist class denounced by the president's distant cousin Theodore as "malefactors of great wealth."

Cultural encounters reinforced the messages of the political finger-pointing, with novels and movies depicting business-men as shallow, selfish, crude, and, worst of all, pathetic. As a precocious teenager, I became fascinated with the Philip Roth stories collected in the book *Goodbye, Columbus* (1959), focus-ing particularly on the title novella with its portrayal of an os-tentatiously prosperous and incurably crude Jewish family in suburban New Jersey, presented by Roth with a toxic, tangy mixture of condescension, compassion, and outright contempt. I saw *The Graduate* a half dozen times within a year of its 1967 release, imputing great profundity to its jaded view of faithless, upper-middle-class hypocrites, afflicted by their materialistic lives. When the Dustin Hoffman character receives a single por-tentous word of advice for his future from a friend of his parents, and that word turns out to be *plastics,* the scene spoke to count-less Americans of my generation about the worthless aspects of the synthetic destiny we sought to avoid. In 1973, *Save the Tiger* (with an Oscar-winning performance by Jack Lemmon) made another deep impression on me, showing the doomed, dysfunc-tional values (and shattering family) of a driven but unfulfilled small businessman, struggling mightily to keep his exploitative clothing business afloat.

For more than a generation, the Hollywood dream factory has continued to churn out similar nightmares that emphasize the ugliest, most unpleasant elements of the commercial, com-petitive system—the same system exemplified, in a particularly ferocious form, by the entertainment industry itself. Despite the fact that the major studios and production companies op-erate as part of international conglomerates that constitute the

"CORRUPTION IS WHY WE WIN!"

The eloquent Gordon Gekko hardly stands alone in winning Oscar attention for films that highlight unethical, irresponsible behavior in the business world. The most common template for such entertainments involves some unlikely, underdog hero or heroine (generally played by a glamorous star, of course) digging deep for unexpected reserves of courage and pluck to do battle against some evil, all-powerful corporation. In *Norma Rae* (1979), Sally Field stands up against a corrupt, rapacious, union-busting textile mill; in *The Verdict* (1982), Paul Newman stands up against the corrupt, rapacious health care industry; in *Silkwood* (1983), Meryl Streep stands up against a corrupt, rapacious nuclear power company; in *A Civil Action* (1998), John Travolta stands up against corrupt, rapacious conglomerates associated with a polluting Massachusetts tannery; in *American Beauty* (1999), Kevin Spacey stands up against the corrupt, rapacious values of his supposed suburban paradise (and his corrupt, faithless realtor wife); in *The Insider* (1999), Al Pacino *and* Russell Crowe stand up against a corrupt, rapacious tobacco company. Just in time for the upcoming market meltdown, 2007 brought two business-bashing Oscar nominees for Best Picture. In *Michael Clayton,* George Clooney stands up (somewhat reluctantly) to a corrupt, rapacious agricultural-chemical company, but in *There Will Be Blood* no one can possibly stand up to Daniel Day-Lewis, a flamboyantly villainous monster who becomes a wealthy 1920s oil tycoon by overwhelming everything else on screen (including the handsomely photographed natural scenery). Lewis won the Best Actor Academy Award for his ferocious performance as an implacably evil entrepreneur (and fulfilling the prophecy "There Will Be Oscars"), and George Clooney won Best Supporting Actor in 2005 for his role as a disillusioned CIA operative in yet another condemnation of corporations, *Syriana*. In this unapologetically anti-American film, U.S. oil companies represent the ultimate source of cruelty and injustice on the planet, and earn even less sympathetic treatment than the CIA or blissfully determined, suicidal jihadists. Tim Blake Nelson plays an energy executive whose corrosive cynicism seems designed to make Gordon Gekko seem idealistic and pure-hearted. Rather than praising greed, Nelson's character hails the power of corruption itself: "Corruption is our protection," he helpfully explains. "Corruption keeps us safe and warm. Corruption is why you and I are prancing around in here instead of fighting over scraps of meat out in the streets. Corruption is why we win!"

most powerful elements of show business, the values and practices of business in general seldom receive sympathetic treatment on screen.

One of the nastiest of all cinematic indictments of corporate corruption, *Wall Street* (1987), was released by one of the largest of all entertainment corporations, 20th Century Fox. Writer-director Oliver Stone contributed the line "Greed is good," endlessly cited to prove the guilt and excess of the 1980s (or any other era that offends political correctness with its emphasis on profit and growth). Even sophisticated journalists and politicos who ought to know better shamelessly quote "Greed is good" as if it represented an authentic, shameful, and revealing capitalist credo, just as they sometimes treat the crooked but charismatic character who pronounced the famous words, Gordon Gekko, as though he represented some iconic historical figure who deserves perpetual denunciation for his ruthless behavior. As recently as October 8, 2008 (more than two decades after the movie's release), Australian prime minister Kevin Rudd reacted to the very real financial crisis with a major address entitled "The Children of Gordon Gekko," declaring, "It is perhaps time now to admit that we did not learn the full lessons of the greed-is-good ideology. And today we are still cleaning up the mess of the 21st-century children of Gordon Gekko."

The prime minister surely knows that Gordon Gekko (note Oliver Stone's choice of the cunningly reptilian last name) enjoyed no more actual existence than James Bond or Dracula or Sherlock Holmes: it's become so convenient to blame this arrogant, appalling financier for every disaster with the market system that we desperately want to believe in him. Gekko's infamous celebration of greed was only loosely inspired by a 1986 speech by the soon-to-be disgraced financier Ivan Boesky, where he told an audience at the University of California, Berkeley, "I think greed is healthy. You can be greedy and still feel good about yourself." Such words certainly lacked the force of the lizard man's invented exhortation (especially as delivered by Michael Douglas in his Oscar-winning performance): "The point is, ladies and gentlemen, that greed, for lack of a better word, is good. Greed is right. Greed works. Greed clarifies, cuts through, and captures the essence of the evolutionary spirit. Greed, in all of its forms—greed for life, for money, for love, knowledge—has marked the upward surge of mankind, and greed—you mark my words—will not only save Teldar Paper but that other malfunctioning corporation called the USA."

BITING THE HAND THAT *IS* YOU

Why would Hollywood, dominated by a handful of shame-lessly capitalistic conglomerates, regularly trash the free-market system, which allowed American media companies to conquer the globe? For movie directors, TV producers, and Tinseltown stars, all of whom have benefited spectacularly from the business of entertainment, this isn't merely an ex-ample of "biting the hand that feeds you." It's a case of biting the hand that *is* you.

According to Larry Ribstein, who teaches business law at the Illinois College of Law in Champaign, it's not "business per se" that raises the objections of filmmakers but the spe-cific businesspeople who control their projects: "Filmmakers' main problem with capital being in control seems to be that the filmmakers are not." Every writer, director, and actor in Hollywood cherishes stories about cruel, crude, exploitative treatment by lunkheaded executives, and these encounters often represent their only personal experience in the world of business. As many entertainment insiders will concede, the vicious, selfish caricatures of corporate bosses that turn up so frequently on TV and in films bear more than a passing resemblance to the studio or network honchos who may have cheated or disappointed the projects' principals in the past.

In part, the ugly view of the corporate system that emerges with such consistency from big corporations in Hol-lywood reflects the distinctively irrational and unpredictable nature of show business. As Academy Award–winning screen-writer William Goldman famously concluded, the operating assumption for the entire industry is "Nobody knows any-thing." In other words, each studio's superhighway of gleam-ing, high-powered can't-miss hits is littered with the twisted wreckage of costly and heartbreaking bombs, while sloppy stinkers that deserve neither respect nor affection often star-tle their own creators by earning inexplicable millions. Unlike the widget-manufacturing business, the entertainment assem-bly line uniquely lacks any objective criterion of excellence. Every actor or actress, no matter how accomplished, realizes at the deepest level that his or her popularity owes as much to a winning smile or burning blue eyes as to painstakingly de-veloped thespian skill.

The rewards of Hollywood, in other words, flow to studio executives and to the creative community alike in a random, fickle, and manifestly unfair manner, which leads pop culture powerhouses to assume that capitalism at large is similarly random, fickle, and unfair. The chronically complaining cre-ative class in Hollywood therefore recycles these destructive distortions and poisons the perceptions of the public.

CYNICAL STORY LINES

In the two decades since doctor Gekko's notorious diagnosis of the nation itself as "a malfunctioning corporation," the leaders of the television industry have joined their movie counterparts in fingering the sleazy businessman as the source of America's problems. Some of the most acclaimed series of recent years (*Arrested Development, Mad Men, The Sopranos*) emphasized the corruption and desolation of amoral power seekers who placed the pursuit of profit above human values. Such cynical story lines have characterized the tube's portrayal of commercial culture for more than a generation. In their 1994 book *Prime Time: How TV Portrays American Culture,* S. Robert Lichter, Linda S. Lichter, and Stanley Rothman, principals of the nonprofit Center for Media and Public Affairs, analyzed thirty years of network television shows. They concluded that across the three decades of their study, "business characters were consistently depicted more negatively than those in other occupations. . . . The proportion of bad guy businessmen is almost double that of all other occupations. . . . Businessmen are over three times more likely to be criminals than are members of other occupations. . . . Although businessmen represent 12 percent of all characters in census-coded occupations, they commit 40 percent of the murders and 44 percent of vice crimes like drug trafficking and pimping."

The scope of the Lichter study (from the presumably less cynical era of the mid-1960s to the date of its completion some fifteen years ago) destroys the claim that lurid portrayals of corporate executives represent an appropriate and inevitable response to the devastation of the 2008 financial meltdown or other economic crises of the recent past. Attempts to quantify the treatment of business characters demonstrate that even in eras of prosperity and progress the portrayal of the business world remained relentlessly and consistently disapproving.

The television news departments affiliated with these same entertainment conglomerates powerfully and predictably reinforce the negative messages about the capitalist system. The Business and Media Institute sponsored a yearlong study of evening news programming on ABC, CBS, NBC, CNN, and Fox, monitoring the treatment of business issues between January 1

"SHOWY MATERIALISM: IT'S A GOOD THING"

Television networks and movie companies celebrate business tycoons as examples of success at the same time that they sneer at them as symbols of excess. The odd association between real estate titan Donald Trump and NBC represents an especially potent instance of this ambivalence. As executive producer and star of his own reality show, *The Apprentice,* since 2003, Trump receives a reported $3 million per episode, making him one of the nation's highest-paid television personalities. Meanwhile, news coverage on the network (and especially on its cable news division, MSNBC) regularly indicts high-flying, heavily leveraged operators like Trump for their role in recent economic disasters. In the *New York Times Magazine* of March 29, 2009, Deborah Solomon pointedly asked The Donald about his place in the new financial universe. "What if your style of showy materialism has become passé?" she demanded.

Without hesitation, Trump confidently (and persuasively) replied, "Great apartments and homes and things of extreme luxury will never be out of fashion. That's what people aspire to. It's a good thing, because it makes people work in order to attain that lifestyle."

and December 31, 2006. Amazingly, in nearly two-thirds (63 percent) of all business stories, business men or women never appeared to comment, even briefly. In those stories, a clear majority, 57 percent (481 of 848), featured negative treatment of the commercial figures involved, employing terms like "corporate fat cats" or "crooks heading to the slammer." The most popular attacks centered on monetary transgressions: unfair pricing, overly lavish CEO pay, or "obscene" corporate profits.

The bitterly negative portrayals of business ethics and accomplishment continue to bombard the public, unaccompanied by contrasting or countervailing visions of heroism or dynamism in the corporate world—a surprising imbalance, considering that the source of all these entertainments remains one of the most ruthlessly competitive and globally consequential of all U.S. enterprises.

"I'M OKAY, BUT YOU'RE IN A WORLD OF HURT AND TROUBLE"

The mass audience of ordinary Americans generally accepts these stereotypical visions of corporate America in spite of personal knowledge to the contrary. Though every citizen cherishes at least a few horrifying or amusing stories about egotistical and abusive bosses, the overall levels of job satisfaction in the United States remain shockingly high. In his indispensable 2008 book *Gross National Happiness,* my friend Arthur Brooks of Syracuse University and the American Enterprise Institute collates a huge volume of data to reveal the underlying American attitudes toward work. "*Dilbert* cartoons, the sitcom *The Office,* and Barbara Ehrenreich's bestselling book *Nickel and Dimed* notwithstanding, Americans like or even love their jobs," he writes. "Among adults who worked ten hours a week or more in 2002, an amazing 89 percent said they were very satisfied or somewhat satisfied with their jobs."

What's more, this overwhelming sense of contentment with their participation in the economic system cuts across all distinctions between blue-collar and white-collar, between the privileged and the powerless. "There is no difference at all in job satisfaction between those with below- and above-average incomes: Eighty-nine percent are satisfied in both groups. Similarly, 88 percent of people without a college education are satisfied. And people who specifically call themselves working class, those 'nickel-and-dimed' folks? Eighty-seven percent. The middle class, who television pundits and politicians say are so increasingly dispirited, are satisfied with their jobs as well, to the tune of 93 percent."

Since many, if not most, of these respondents pursue their employment in the business world, these upbeat attitudes appear to contradict the surveys that show overwhelmingly negative views of business executives. How could Americans report such high levels of pride and pleasure in their jobs when they express so little respect for the ethics or honor of the big shots for whom they toil?

The answer involves a media-driven syndrome that spreads confusion in every corner of American life. Forty years ago Thomas Harris published *I'm OK, You're OK,* one of the best-selling self-help books in the history of civilization. Unfortunately, most members of the public now embrace a very different concept—"I'm okay, but you're in a world of hurt and trouble." The great majority of people say they're hugely pleased with their own family life, for instance, but then declare (by similarly huge margins) that the general state of the family is dire and desperate. Most parents express pride and satisfaction with their own children's public schools but assume that the rest of the education system does a horrible job. Voters overwhelmingly re-elect their own Representatives in Congress but tell pollsters that Congress on the whole counts as a disgrace; they love their doctors and feel pleased (some 77 percent!) with their health insurance, but still assume that the system itself is broken and needs radical change.

The chief cause of these contradictions involves the common reliance on media for information about the world beyond personal experience. The individual American never counts on Brian Williams (or his colleagues) to assess the state of his or her own marriage, health, or financial well-being, but uses the images and messages from television to evaluate the situation in society at large. Inevitably, the media reports always emphasize dysfunction and difficulty and despair—tornadoes get better ratings than sunshine, and torture-murder attracts more attention than acts of kindness or philanthropy. The networks and newspapers (as well as the new medium of the Internet) don't constitute a news business as much as they function as a *bad* news business. When we acknowledge our blessings, and revel in our own freakishly fortunate lives, we become convinced that we're far removed from our neighbors—surviving on a tiny sun-kissed island of good fortune surrounded by turbulent and toxic oceans of despair. In the world of business, we assume that the respectable head of our company stands apart from all his colleagues rather than challenge the prevailing assumptions about the corporate system itself. Regarding our jobs, or our children's teachers, or our elected representatives or our physicians, we conclude that we've secured the only good and wholesome apples in a vast barrel crammed with rotten fruit.

GRATITUDE ABOVE GUILT

The prevailing view of a dysfunctional and desperate business system flows from widely accepted, endlessly repeated lies that directly conflict with the actual economic engagement of most Americans.

The crucial lies insist

- that capitalism and the free-market system are dead— or dying
- that when the rich get richer, the poor get poorer
- that business executives receive gross overpayment for empty, lazy, corrupt, and unproductive lives
- that big business, with its global reach, is inherently worse for both consumers and workers than small business
- that government responds to public needs more reliably and more compassionately than the private sector

These pillars of conventional wisdom go largely unchallenged in academia and the media, where various experts and traditional critics of the free market eagerly emphasize the bad news about business. Nevertheless, many Americans feel instinctive doubt or at least discomfort with the ubiquitous smears against an economic system that allows us to plan, produce, and dream. This book aims to provide both arguments and information to counter the distortions that warp perceptions about American business.

Despite more than a century of socialist agitation aiming to purge "selfish" motives from every aspect of our society, we still rely on for-profit companies in every moment of our lives. I couldn't be writing these words without the computer company that produced the word-processing program, or the publishers who printed my sources, or the coffee distributor who provided brewed fortification. Even if you toil at some supposedly noble nonprofit enterprise, every element of your job depends on some productive capitalist venture—from the car (or bike or bus) that took you to work, to the lights and phones and desks and electricity essential to any office, to the building itself, to the food and plates and glasses in the lunchroom. For entertainment, we're utterly dependent on the competitive business system—to organize a nice restaurant, or a good movie at the local multiplex, or a trendy club, or a major-league baseball game (and think of all the companies that worked on that scoreboard with its jumbotron, or the retractable roof, or the increasingly exotic fare available between innings, or the exercise equipment that trains the athletes, or their beautifully crafted mitts and bats and cleats).

One could argue that we only avoid the blessings of business in those hours that we manage to sleep, but even then we need someone to provide the bed, and sheets, and pillows, and alarm clock, and heating, and windows with screens, and red wine (or Ambien, if you're so inclined) when needed. The literally hundreds of thousands of people required to deliver these goods and services may not see themselves as our benefactors, but they help and serve us nonetheless.

The satisfaction of each of our needs in daily life requires processes of overwhelming complexity that for-profit business provides in seemingly effortless, organic fashion. The companies that serve themselves by serving others manage to bind us together in an intricate system of demand and fulfillment. The pursuit of profit allows us to depend on one another and to build those ongoing connections of mutual benefit that are the very essence of community.

The notion that the exchange of money poisons human relationships defies both logic and experience. Consider the connection between employer and employee—two people, one of whom pays the other a regular, mutually agreed-upon fee for support and assistance. Compare that association with a romantic link between two passionately infatuated individuals, and ask which relationship is likely to qualify as more honest, open, flexible, stable, and, in the long term, mutually rewarding. The fact that both parties to a capitalist connection stand to gain from it is an advantage for such associations, not an indictment. At the same time the unselfishness and sacrifice often associated with love connections, or with the links between an adored leader and his devoted followers, may make those relationships suspect rather than superior.

Far from the heart-hardening and spirit-killing processes cited by poets or movie producers who loudly lament the central role of business in our society, the capitalist system actually opens us to a greater sense of connection, community, and even creativity. When an eager public willingly delivers financial rewards to a productive talent who's provided joy or inspiration, both audience and artist feel uplifted by the transaction. There's nothing especially honorable about a novelist or painter starving in a garret, or relying on government grants, rather than selling his work at a handsome profit to those who value it. The great British musician Gustav Holst (1874–1934), the supremely gifted composer of *The Planets,* once declared, "Only a second rate artist can afford to be unbusinesslike."

Businesspeople—particularly those who defy the odds and launch their own companies—are builders by nature, and the work of building expresses the essence of creativity. I should have taken more time to recognize these shaping, imaginative,

A PRESIDENTIAL PUT-DOWN
OF THE PROFIT MOTIVE

In the midst of the economic crisis of 2009, some of the nation's most prominent politicians expressed wrongheaded hostility to the profit motive that will play a necessary role in any potential recovery. On May 13, President Obama addressed the graduates of Arizona State University and told them that "the old order has been shaken, the old ideas and institutions have crumbled, and a new generation is called upon to remake the world." In his bitter description of those "old ideas," the leader of the Free World lavished special scorn on traditional dreams of upward mobility, suggesting that they actually displayed "a poverty of ambition."

"Now, in the face of these challenges, it may be tempting to fall back on the formulas for success that have been peddled so frequently in recent years," the president declaimed. "It goes something like this: You're taught to chase after all the usual brass rings; you try to be on this 'who's who' list or that top 100 list; you chase after the big money and you figure out how big your corner office is; you worry about whether you have a fancy enough title or a fancy enough car. That's the message that's sent each and every day, or has been in our culture for far too long—that through material possessions, through a ruthless competition pursued only on your own behalf—that's how you will measure success."

As Fred Barnes aptly commented in *The Weekly Standard,* "That's a brutal caricature of the way most people seek to get ahead in life, support a family and gain financial security."

Near the end of his speech, President Obama specifically

addressed those presumably benighted graduates who had made the mistake of pursuing degrees in business. "You have no excuses not to change the world. Did you study business? Go start a company. Or why not help our struggling non-profits find better, more effective ways to serve folks in need." The tone of his warmly received remarks made it clear that he viewed nonprofit work (like community organizing) as a higher calling than involvement in the corporate world of "ruthless competition" for which the business students had trained. He simultaneously ignored the fact that pursuit of profit and tireless business-building bring rising levels of national and international prosperity that "serve folks in need" far more reliably than even the best-intentioned among "struggling non-profits."

daring qualities in my father's many decades as an independent businessman. It wasn't just scientific breakthroughs that let him relish every day as a new adventure, nor was it the satisfaction of profit and financial progress (unfortunately, he did not die a wealthy man). He loved the sense of initiation and assembly, nourishing institutions that grew out of his own energy and imagination, turning out nifty high-tech products that no one had ever shaped before. He also savored the relationships, with colleagues, employees, even competitors. He treasured the vision of his companies as busy little independent villages he had founded, with their own distinctive cultures and traditions, with all the industrious townspeople (who invariably admired him) working for a common purpose.

He didn't have time for the prevailing slanders and distortions of the free-market system and so simply disregarded and discredited them with his example. Instead of debating the big lies about American business, he lived the big truths. We never spoke about the contents of this book but I feel confident that he would applaud its effort to place the pursuit of profit in appropriate perspective. Even at a time of financial hardship and menace, a celebration of the resilience and logic of democratic capitalism will make it easier to face the challenges ahead with inspiration rather than insecurity, and with gratitude above guilt.

"The Current Downturn Means the Death of Capitalism"

Time to Butcher

1912, by socialist cartoonist Art Young

"A FINE OLD CONFLICT"

For the better part of five generations, the enemies of capitalism have been singing lustily to celebrate its imminent demise.

During strikes, demonstrations, May Day parades, and other sacred occasions, those who reject and denounce the free-market system still raise their clenched fists and solemnly intone the thrilling words of "The Internationale," worldwide anthem of the socialist and Communist movements:

No more tradition's chains shall bind us,
Arise you slaves no more in thrall!
The earth shall rise on new foundations
We have been nought, we shall be all!

'Tis the final conflict,
Let each stand in his place
The international soviet
Shall be the human race!
'Tis the final conflict,
Let each stand in his place
The international working class
Shall be the human race!

As a young teenager in London, Jessica Mitford accompanied her governess to Hyde Park for regular Sunday expeditions to savor radical soapbox oratory and fervent renditions of this song. Unfortunately, she mistook the repeated references to "the final conflict" for an invocation of a "fine old conflict." In fact, she later gave the title *A Fine Old Conflict* to a wry 1977 memoir of her decades-long affiliation with the Communist Party.

For Mitford and other critics of the free-market system, their ongoing conflict with capitalism may indeed count as "fine" and "old" but it's never come close to climactic finality.

The florid text of "The Internationale" came from the pen of transport worker and revolutionary leader Eugène Pottier in June 1871, two weeks after the collapse of the sixty-day socialist

THE "TRUTH" BURIES CAPITALISM

Twenty years ago, American advocates for the free market congratulated themselves on the collapse of Russian Communism, so there was an inevitable sense of score-settling in 2009 when Russian Communists congratulated themselves on the collapse of American capitalism. On April 27, the online newspaper Pravda, successor to the official Communist Party organ that dominated Soviet media for eighty years, ran a prominent editorial under the headline "American Capitalism, Gone with a Whimper."

"It must be said, that like the breaking of a great dam, the American descent into Marxism is happening with breathtaking speed, against the backdrop of a passive, hapless sheeple—excuse me, dear reader, I meant people," declared the unsigned commentary. The great majority of today's *Pravda* staffers once worked for the old official publication (before its forced closure by President Yeltsin in 1991) and they have maintained their vitriolic anti-Americanism, if not their doctrinal Marxist purity.

Their "death of capitalism" editorial denounced U.S. citizens who "care more about their 'right' to choke down a McDonald's burger or a Burger King burger than their Constitutional rights.... Then their faith in God was destroyed, until their churches, all tens of thousands of different branches and denominations, were for the most part little more than circuses and their televangelists and top Protestant megapreachers were more than happy to sell out their souls and flocks to be on the 'winning' side of one pseudo-Marxist politician or another.... The final collapse has come with the election of Barack Obama. His speed in the past three months has been truly impressive. His spending and money printing has been record-setting, not just in America's short history but in the world. If this keeps up for more than another year, and there is no sign that it will not, America at best will resemble the Weimar Republic and at worst Zimbabwe."

The gleeful reporting on misfortunes and changes in the United States, and particularly on the perceived abandonment of the nation's traditional pro-business attitudes, echoed the glory days of *Pravda,* when the paper regularly trumpeted progress in the worldwide Bolshevik struggle against the capitalist West. In Russian, *pravda* means "truth," and *izvestia* (the name of the official newspaper of the Soviet government, as opposed to the Communist Party) means "news." This gave rise to a popular saying by the cynical citizens of the old Soviet Union: "In the *Truth* there is no news, and in the *News* there is no truth."

insurrection known as the Paris Commune. Despite the bloody breakdown of his utopian dreams, Pottier felt exhilarated by his personal participation in street fighting amidst the boulevard barricades; as he poetically proclaimed in his celebrated song, "Justice thunders condemnation: a better world's in birth!"

For a hundred forty years, Pottier's fellow visionaries have eagerly awaited that promised delivery, expecting the rapid unraveling of the profit-motive economic system that ultimately reached its most powerful, influential expression in the United States of America. Even among the reigning elites of that bourgeois Republic, young radicals of the 1960s believed that their own insurrectionary adventures in the Ivy League could bring the nation's business crashing to a halt. Even at the time, it struck some of us as insanely narcissistic to expect that a boycott of classes or the occupation of administration buildings by a few self-righteous students at Harvard, Columbia, or Yale would threaten the productivity and progress of the most prosperous economy in the history of the world.

"STAND ATHWART HISTORY YELLING . . . 'WE LOST!' "

A generation later, the apocalyptic assumptions of a few expensively educated radicals may seem adolescent, idiotic, and altogether unwarranted, but no more so, surely, than the ubiquitous proclamations of capitalism's demise by the heavy-breathing doomsayers of Left and Right in our very own Age of Obama. Shortly after the presidential election of 2008, filmmaker Michael Moore appeared on *Larry King Live* on CNN to announce a transition of cosmic importance: "And I think, really, what we're seeing now, we're seeing the end of capitalism," cackled the portly provocateur. "The end of capitalism as we know it and I say good riddance. It hasn't helped the people or the planet."

On a similar note, *Newsweek* ran a notorious cover story (February 16, 2009), coauthored by its editor, Jon Meacham, under the headline "We Are All Socialists Now," suggesting a new consensus regarding the demise of the free-market economy. A few months later (June 2), *USA Today* columnist Jonah Goldberg aptly pointed out that even Meacham himself had quickly abandoned the claim of socialism's universal acceptance and returned to the idea that in the United States describing someone with the S-word still represented a savage insult. In an adoring interview with President Obama, Meacham snickered over nasty right-wing suggestions that the leader of the Free World actually qualified as a "crypto-socialist."

Actually, conservatives went much further than that, rarely bothering with the timid qualifier "crypto." On March 23, *National Review* ran a cover story under the headline "Our Socialist Future." The magazine William Buckley founded to "stand athwart history yelling, 'Stop'" instead seemed oddly (and briefly) resigned to stand aside sighing, "We lost." Glenn Beck, lachrymose and theatrical host of a popular program on the Fox News channel, planned a new book entitled "America's March to Socialism" and often illustrated his TV show with archival footage of goose-stepping hordes in Red Square, Beijing, or Nazi Berlin. Senator Jim DeMint, the stalwart Republican from South Carolina, offered his own book of dire observations about Obamanism but sounded a slightly more optimistic tone in his title: "Saving Freedom: We Can Stop America's Slide into Socialism."

Inevitably, the apocalyptic overreaction to President Obama's unrestrained deficit spending and grandiose big-government schemes spread from pundits and politicians to grassroots activists, who flooded town hall meetings on health care reform with signs and chants proclaiming the imminent arrival of socialism, fascism, or some other form of unspeakable tyranny.

In a thoughtful April 2 column in the *Wall Street Journal,* the always insightful Daniel Henninger asked the dreaded question "Is this the end of capitalism?" and then answered his own query with a resounding no, explaining, "Capitalism didn't tank

"CAPITALISM WILL FAIL"—AND COST $17,000 IN TUITION

Each year, Black Pine Circle School, which serves children between kindergarten and eighth grade in Berkeley, California, invites students to contribute to a class mosaic, prominently displayed at the entrance to the campus. At the end of the 2008–2009 academic year, some of the precocious middle-schoolers came up with the idea of announcing the doom of the free-market economic system.

The school's seventh- and eighth-graders created and posted a series of brightly painted tiles featuring the hammer-and-sickle symbol of international Communism and bearing the cheerful message "Capitalism Will Fail."

"Being Berkeley, of course, we don't censor their creative expression," said Laura Wolff, assistant director of the august academic institution. "It's fun to see what they come up with." According to its website, the Black Pine Circle School makes sure that all its students will be "maximally free of all the 'isms' which pervade most aspects of the world around them, from racism to sexism to the less obvious forms of discrimination."

Obviously, "social-ism" and "commun-ism" didn't count among the banned "isms" for the BPCS community. While the students dreamed of a classless society free of the evil profit motive, they left it to their parents, no doubt the brutalized victims of savage capitalist exploitation, to come up with tuition of $17,100.

the U.S. economy. Overbuilt housing did. Overbuilt housing tanked the economies of the U.K. and Ireland and Spain." Unfortunately, millions saw the alarming headline, but far fewer read the reassuring content of his piece.

"ONLY A MATTER OF TIME . . ."

All the dire and portentous talk about the current "crisis of capitalism" carries with it an inescapably familiar, even shopworn feel for those acquainted with recent history. In the "Camelot" era of 1962, African-American activist Malcom X unequivocally announced, "It is impossible for capitalism to survive, primarily because the system of capitalism needs some blood to suck. Capitalism used to be like an eagle, but now it's more like a vulture. . . . It's only a matter of time in my opinion before it will collapse completely."

During the Great Depression, of course, some of the finest minds of the century expected the weakened economic system to disappear altogether. On the eve of FDR's 1933 inauguration, theologian Reinhold Niebuhr offered an obituary for the old order, written on the assumption that "capitalism is dying and with the conviction that it ought to die." A member of Congress expressed similar sentiments the same year: Tom Amlie, a Wisconsin Republican who later returned to the House as a representative of the Progressive Party, told a convention of radicals that the system had no future because Roosevelt wouldn't spend the huge sums necessary to "keep it alive." In any event, he declared that "whether capitalism could be kept going for another period of years or not, it is not worth saving."

A more influential figure of that era, three-term Minnesota governor Floyd Bjørnstjerne Olson, made the destruction of capitalism even more central to his political persona. When asked by visiting journalists whether he considered himself "radical," the populist governor with the booming voice and larger-than-life personality liked to shock them by announcing, "I'm radical as hell!" In 1934, he addressed the convention of his Farmer-Labor Association (the ancestor of today's Democratic Farmer Labor Party in Minnesota) and explained that he felt tired of "tinkering and patching" and wanted to change the entire business system in his state. The convention obliged by adopting a platform that specifically declared that "capitalism has failed and that immediate steps must be taken by the people to abolish capitalism in a peaceful and lawful manner, and that a new, sane, and just society must be established; a system in which all the natural resources, machinery of production, transportation and communication shall be owned by the government." Despite the extreme rhetoric of the platform, Olson won reelection in a landslide. He toyed with the notion of challenging FDR from the left as a third-party candidate in 1936, but rejected the idea shortly before he died in office of stomach cancer. He was only forty-four, and remains a wildly popular figure in Minnesota history and folklore.

In the 1930s, the assumption that the free-market system must quickly fall to pieces became so widespread that intellectuals concentrated many of their arguments on selecting the most promising replacement. Lawrence Dennis, former child evangelist, first lieutenant in World War I, and Foreign Service officer, passionately rejected both the Communist and socialist alternatives. Instead, he became one of the nation's most influential advocates for fascism in the style of Hitler or Mussolini. In a letter to a friend he wrote, "I should like nothing better than to be a leader or a follower of a Hitler who would crush or destroy many now in power." In 1932 he published an influential and much-discussed book, *Is Capitalism Doomed?*, and then answered his own question with his next release, in 1936, *The Coming American Fascism.*

IRRESISTIBLE TIDES OF HISTORY

For many reasons, the commentators, activists, and politicians of the 1930s had far more basis for predicting the end of the free-market system than either gloomy conservatives or gleeful leftists in 2009. Most significantly, as the arguments of Lawrence Dennis made clear, developments around the world suggested that the irresistible tides of history favored an international future of statism. With the unholy trinity of Hitler, Mussolini, and Stalin riding high in Eurasia the capitalist institutions of the United States looked increasingly isolated—even as modified and rearranged and regulated by FDR. Aside from the growing domain of the dictators, huge swaths of the globe had not yet developed modern capitalist economies that radicals could reject. China remained paralyzed by a chilling combination of colonialism (both Western and Japanese), feudalism, and warlordism, with Mao's rebellion already gaining considerable strength. The Japanese Empire ran according to principles of medieval militarism, rejecting the Western profit system as soft and corrupt. India remained the "crown jewel" of the British Empire, with only the bare rudiments of business development, while colonialism continued to dominate the lives of the vast majority of people in Asia and Africa, with corrupt kleptocracies all but universal in Latin America. Only Canada and a small handful of Western European nations shared the values or economic outlook of the United States, and every year the forces of collectivism and dictatorship seemed to gain strength and influence.

By contrast, the thirty years preceding the economic crisis of 2008–2009 displayed unstoppable momentum in the opposite direction. The embrace of free-market ideals became so universal that Francis Fukuyama famously proclaimed "the end of history" in 1992, arguing that the long dispute between capitalism and authoritarian socialism had been settled in favor of free markets and democratic institutions. The world's two most populous nations, China and India, both pursued radical economic reforms to empower the for-profit private economy and reduce central planning (and control) of the economy. The results for both nations involved unimaginably spectacular and consistent growth, and an unprecedented improvement in living standards for nearly half of humanity. China implacably resisted the long-awaited political reforms to accompany its booming economy, and Russia flirted with one-party rule and showed scant respect for civil liberties, but both nations engaged the world economy in distinctly capitalist terms. Putin's Russia even experimented (mostly successfully) with a flat tax, a startling development that should encourage free-marketeers everywhere. Other former Communist bloc nations of Eastern and Central Europe not only flocked to join the European Union and NATO but also developed some of the most vibrant capitalist economies on earth.

Fareed Zakaria, of CNN and *Newsweek,* effectively summarized the advances of the last generation: "Over the past quarter century, the global economy has doubled every 10 years, going from $31 trillion in 1999 to $62 trillion in 2008. Recessions have become tamer than ever before, averaging eight months rather than two years. More than 400 million people across Asia have been lifted out of poverty. Between 2003 and 2007, average income worldwide grew at a faster rate (3.1 percent) than in any previous period in recorded human history. In 2006 and 2007— the peak years of the boom—124 countries around the world grew at 4 percent a year or more, about four times as many as 25 years earlier."

Far from the steep, unstoppable "slide into socialism" jointly heralded by gloom-and-doom conservatives and overconfident Obamanaut apostles of hope-and-change, the decades before the crash actually brought a steady ascent toward democratic capitalism that permanently altered political and economic realities around the world.

"SIMPLE, NEAT, AND WRONG"

The crisis of 2008–2009 may have stalled this progress but in no sense erased it, or discredited the system that produced it. The most astute observers cite the long history of financial crisis and remind the dispirited public that business cycles count as inevitable, even healthy. Niall Ferguson, the brilliant professor at Harvard and the Harvard Business School (writing in the *New York Times Magazine,* May 17, 2009) recalled other burst bubbles that loomed as apocalyptic and world-shattering to the societies they afflicted: "In the early 1340s, a sovereign-debt crisis wiped out the leading Florentine banks of Bardi, Peruzzi and

Acciaiuoli. Between December 1719 and December 1720, the price of shares of John Law's Mississippi Company fell 90 percent. Such crashes can also happen to real estate: in Japan, property prices fell by more than 60 percent during the '90s."

Ferguson faults academics as well as business leaders for failing to learn from such disasters. "For reasons to do with human psychology and the failure of most educational institutions to teach financial history, we are always more amazed when such things happen than we should be. As a result, 9 times out of 10 we overreact. The usual response is to introduce a raft of new laws and regulations designed to prevent the crisis from repeating itself. In the months ahead, the world will reverberate to the sound of stable doors being shut long after the horses have bolted, and history suggests that many of the new measures will do more harm than good."

In the current situation, the most popular, prevalent "new measures" meant to guarantee eternal prosperity illustrate the timeless wisdom in Mencken's observation that "for every complex problem, there is a solution that is simple, neat and wrong." In the United States, the president and his media supporters insist that *de*-regulation caused the present predicament and that *re*-regulation will preclude future catastrophes. Professor Ferguson takes a dim view of these nostrums for three potent reasons. First, deregulation gathered its most formidable momentum several decades ago—with the Depository Institutions Deregulation and Monetary Control Act that cleared Congress under President Carter in 1980, and other dramatic measures that followed under President Reagan. These reforms involved far more sweeping changes than any of the tinkering undertaken by the Bushes or Clinton, so if cutting back on bureaucratic guidelines leads directly to economic chaos, then the recent collapse arrived at least twenty years too late. As Ferguson argues, "If deregulation is to blame for the recession that began in December 2007, presumably it should also get some of the credit for the intervening growth."

The second problem with advocating tighter governmental rules as potent protection against future falls involves the abject failure of such regulations in the past. Ferguson notes that the "much greater financial regulation of the 1970s" did nothing to prevent the toxic combination of double-digit inflation and a devastating recession (1973–75) "every bit as severe as the one we're in now."

Finally, there's the international perspective: European governments impose far more rigorous rules and restrictions on their financial sectors than does the United States, but they have suffered even worse disruptions in their banking systems. The political class in Germany indignantly disapproves of the "Anglo-Saxon" financial model employed by the Americans and the British, but 2008 bank leverage was four times higher in Germany than in the United States. Two weeks after Ferguson's analysis, worldwide economic figures underscored his point. Under the headline "World Economies Plummet," the *Wall Street Journal* reported on the sharp declines of gross domestic product for the first quarter of 2009. While GDP in the United States, with its purportedly fatal lack of regulation, plunged by 6.3 percent, the tightly planned and rules-bound economies of Germany and Japan retreated more than twice as quickly, losing 14.4 percent and 15.2 percent, respectively. The near-universal pain of the current recession hardly suggests that American policy makers could have escaped the downturn by emulating the example of our even more deeply distressed European allies.

"A VERY DIFFICULT EVENING
FOR SOCIALISTS"

As it happened, that widespread continental distress contributed to an electoral earthquake in the first weekend of June 2009, exploding the smug assumption that worldwide economic crisis would lead inevitably to a global slide toward socialism. Balloting for the European Parliament expressed a continent-wide rejection of left-wing economic prescriptions, with center-right parties crushing their socialist opponents nearly everywhere (except Greece). In France, Germany, Italy, and Belgium, ruling center-right coalitions strengthened their standing, while the opposition conservatives in Britain, Spain, Portugal, the Netherlands, and most of Eastern Europe gained significant ground. The *Wall Street Journal* chortled in reaction: "Across the Continent, the left is in disarray." On election night, Martin Schulz, leader of the socialists in the European Parliament, frankly acknowledged, "Tonight is a very difficult evening for Socialists in many nations in Europe." Hungary provided an especially dramatic example of the emphatic rejection of the Left. Candidates of the ruling Socialist Party drew only 17 percent of the vote, while the right-wing opposition party gained 56 percent (and a far-right anti-Gypsy party earned an additional 15 percent). If the economic crisis meant the inevitable end of the free-market system, voters of the European Union failed to get the memo. Despite the grim talk of an all-but-inevitable march toward socialism, the recent balloting gives evidences of an international surge *toward* capitalism. In Canada and Israel, market-oriented coalitions also won recent electoral victories, and only in Latin

America (with conspicuous exceptions like Mexico and Colombia) have leftist candidates regularly triumphed.

In contemplating socialism's long-term retreat in the Old World, leftist economist Robert Kuttner lamented in the Huffington Post, "American progressives used to look longingly to Europe, with its stronger trade unions and its more comprehensive social protections. Those are still there, but unraveling under assault."

Of course, advocates for a more aggressive governmental role could take some comfort from Barack Obama's election in the United States, but the claims that his personal victory represented a watershed choice and a decisive realignment look increasingly tenuous in light of surveys during his first year in office. Throughout the initial summer of Obama's presidency, daily tracking polls by Rasmussen Reports show a sizable, steady lead for those who "strongly disapprove" of the new chief executive's performance over those who "strongly approve." A party identification poll by Gallup showed Republicans and Democrats virtually tied. And "generic congressional ballots" analyzed by Rasmussen and other pollsters forecast a tight battle in House and Senate races of 2010, or even picked up a lead for the GOP.

The outcome of such surveys will shift quickly and unpredictably in the next months and years, but they do indicate that the American people have made no significant ideological shift toward collectivism. Even the president's stratospheric personal popularity in the first weeks of his term failed to produce a reliable majority for the big-government reforms he favored.

In March, the Pew Research Center asked respondents if we are better off "in a free market economy even though there may

"MORE CAPITALISM, NOT LESS"

Just five months after its celebrated cover story "We Are All Socialists Now," *Newsweek* ran a reconsideration (of sorts) under the heading "The Capitalist Manifesto: Greed Is Good (To a Point)." The thoughtful essay by Fareed Zakaria concluded that reports of the demise of the free-market system had been greatly exaggerated: "A few years from now, strange as it may sound, we might all find that we are hungry for more capitalism, not less. An economic crisis slows growth, and when countries need growth they turn to markets. After the Mexican and East Asian currency crises—which were far more painful in those countries than the current downturn has been in America—we saw the pace of market oriented reform speed up. If, in the years ahead, the American consumer remains reluctant to spend, if federal and state governments groan under their debt loads, if government owned companies remain expensive burdens, then private-sector activity will become the only path to create jobs" (June 22, 2009).

be severe ups and downs from time to time." A reassuring 70 percent agreed, while only 20 percent disagreed.

That same month (March 2009) a DDB survey featured in *USA Today* asked the restive and gloomy public to report on the chief lessons from the financial collapse. The largest group (42 percent) described the crisis as "payback for overindulging." An almost identical number (38 percent) said that the hard times "showed me what's important." Meanwhile, a mere 14 percent agreed with the notion that economic reverses "prove that capitalism is bad."

"A LONG, TWILIGHT STRUGGLE"

In the last analysis, the prevalent predictions about the free market's destruction and the coming of a new socialist order amount to a simplistic, childish, ill-informed distortion with unlikely origins in the bad old days of the Cold War.

During the years of "long, twilight struggle" (in JFK's haunting phrase), serious people saw the developed portions of the planet as crisply divided between "The Iron Curtain" and "The Free World," Communist dictatorships versus lands of liberty, them versus us. Some nations insisted on "nonaligned" status (led by poverty-stricken India with its pacifist and neutralist traditions), but even those bastions of indecision ran the horrible risk of "going Communist."

According to the understanding of the time, when any nation "went Communist" and installed puppets of the Soviet Union in positions of real power, the alteration in status became permanent. The Communist agents or dupes might come to power through elections and the manipulation of democratic institutions, but in many countries that meant a quick brutal crackdown on all opposition and the rapid establishment of the mechanics of dictatorship—leading to the wry description "one man, one vote, one time."

Future UN ambassador Jeane Kirkpatrick became famous and won the attention of Ronald Reagan by writing an article ("Dictatorships and Double Standards," November 1979) that talked about the long-term results of Communist takeover. In making the case for the uneasy U.S. alliance with various non-democratic regimes, she emphasized the distinction between "authoritarian" and "totalitarian" dictatorships. In authoritarian nations (like Batista's Cuba) the government never took full control of all institutions and allowed rival sources of power, thereby admitting possibilities for change. In totalitarian regimes (like *Castro's* Cuba) the ruling elite attempted to dominate all political, economic, and cultural institutions, allowing no challenge to its all-inclusive power and providing virtually no chance for change.

According to the conventional wisdom of the time, no totalitarian regime had ever released its oppressed populace or evolved toward enlightenment; such nation-states could be transformed (as with Nazi Germany and Imperial Japan) only through the overwhelming application of military force. This meant that once a society "went Communist," there was no chance to turn back peacefully, and you could count on that nation to work against American interests, follow the Soviet lead, and shun all ideals of liberty and decency.

Such thinking contributed powerfully to the decision to fight both the Korean and the Vietnam Wars, and also impacts the current debate about "our socialist future" and the demise of the free-market system. For many worried conservatives, the possibility that the Obama administration will impose a vast expansion of the federal government amounts to the chance that America would "go socialist," moving definitively and permanently from column A to column B. According to this argument, once the majority of voters grow accustomed to a cornucopia of governmental goodies, it will be impossible to break their addiction, and the irresponsible spending will bring about either the bankruptcy of the federal government or (far more likely) vastly increased and punishing taxes on society's most productive citizens.

The problem with this line of reasoning is that there is no clear or obvious tipping point in which a nation moves permanently from the sunlight of liberty into the shadows of statist tyranny. There's also little historical evidence that even the most radical sorts of bureaucratic expansion amount to irreversible change.

Consider the mother country, our friends across the pond in the British Isles. In the thirty-four years from the end of World War II till the arrival of Margaret Thatcher at 10 Downing Street, the officially socialist Labour Party controlled the government almost precisely half the time. They succeeded in instituting the National Health Service (socialized medicine) and vastly increased spending for public housing and other welfare programs. Did this mean that the United Kingdom had "gone socialist" and couldn't return to a dynamic market economy?

Fortunately, Mrs. Thatcher didn't believe in the inevitable loss of British initiative, and in 1979 she set about transforming her country for the better. She didn't immediately reestablish capitalism any more than her Labour predecessors had firmly established socialism. She did, however, move a mixed economy in a free-market direction, in much the same way that Barack Obama means to push the American economy in a big-government, "spread the wealth," collectivist direction.

All Western nations operate with mixed economies, and the mix is different from place to place and from time to time. Switzerland shares a border with Germany, but the two nations offer vastly different economic and tax systems (so that any true lover of liberty will prefer Swiss chocolate to German beer). Ronald Reagan took over the White House directly from Jimmy Carter but he brought vastly different ideas to the table on how

DOES THE STOCK MARKET CRASH RESEMBLE THE FALL OF THE BERLIN WALL?

No one celebrated the economic crisis more jubilantly than Canadian writer Naomi Klein, bestselling author of *The Shock Doctrine: The Rise of Disaster Capitalism* (2007). She viewed the financial turmoil as a liberating and historic turning point, marking the definitive demise of free-market policies. "What we are seeing with the crash on Wall Street," she declared, "should be for Friedmanism what the fall of the Berlin Wall was for authoritarian communism: an indictment of ideology."

Her analogy suggested an unsupportable equivalence between the brutal Stalinist oligarchs of East Germany and the bookish, soft-spoken, Nobel Prize–winning University of Chicago economist Milton Friedman. While it's true that painful stock market losses might constitute an "indictment of ideology," most sane observers would conclude that 100 million deaths (a conservative estimate of Communism's twentieth-century victims) would reflect even worse on a system of ideas. Concerning the Berlin Wall, East German guards murdered nearly 200 people trying to flee to the West during the twenty-eight years (1961–89) of the barrier's cruel existence. Moreover, anyone who lived through the Cold War will remember that the Soviets and their allies constructed the wall not to keep outsiders away (there was no worldwide lust for visiting East Germany) but to stop their own enslaved citizens from escaping their empire. The United States, on the other hand, struggles with the reality of uncounted millions who yearn to relocate in

America—despite a current population presumably groaning in the shackles of "Friedmanism." Though immigration (both legal and illegal) has certainly declined in the midst of the recession, 1,107,126 authorized newcomers entered the United States in 2008.

to run the nation's bureaucracy and economy (Reagan believed the economy should, ultimately, run itself). Naturally, it makes a difference when a president attempts to lead the nation in a new direction, but the chief impact of his efforts will be to alter the balance (probably only slightly) between the private and public sectors.

The notion that Europe has become a socialist wasteland with no entrepreneurial energy and no possibility of redemption distorts the continent's complicated realities. Russell Shorto, an American writer living in Amsterdam, provided a fascinating account of life in the supposedly "socialist" Netherlands for the *New York Times Magazine.* "It is and has long been a highly capitalistic country," he writes. "The Dutch pioneered the multinational corporation and advanced the concept of shares of stock and last year the country was the third-largest investor in U.S. businesses—and yet it has what I had been led to believe was a vast, socialistic welfare state."

Even the top Dutch tax rate of 52 percent misleads people about one of the Old World's more prosperous enclaves. Noting that the top federal tax rate in the United States now stands at 35 percent, Shorto quotes Constanze Woelfle, an American accountant working in Amsterdam. "People coming from the U.S. to the Netherlands focus on that difference, on that 52 percent," she said. "But consider that the Dutch rate includes social security, which in the U.S. is an additional 6.2 percent. Then in the U.S. you have state and local taxes, and much higher real estate taxes. If you were to add all those up, you could get close to 52 percent."

Even if President Obama raises that figure beyond the Dutch level, the chances for future cuts and reforms remain vibrant. The top tax rate has fluctuated wildly over the years in response to both economic and political pressures—from 73 percent under Woodrow Wilson, to 24 percent under Calvin Coolidge, to 92 percent under Harry Truman, to 70 percent under John Kennedy, to 28 percent under Reagan, and then back to 39.6 percent under Bill Clinton. Though all Americans would benefit from more predictability, rationality, and simplicity in the tax code, there's no reason to assume that the forthcoming rate increases under Barack Obama will be any more permanent than previous alterations.

In fact, the president and his most influential advisers strenuously deny the charge that they seek to impose "a kind of backdoor socialism." Lawrence Summers, director of the National Economic Council (and secretary of the treasury under Bill Clinton), spoke to the Council on Foreign Relations in June 2009 and portrayed his new boss as a "defender of free markets." He assured his eager audience that administration initiatives to rescue banks and auto companies aimed to save capitalism, not to destroy it. "If you take one message from what I say today, take this: Only if government is no longer a major presence in these companies in short order, will we have succeeded in achieving our critical objectives," Summers declared. He insisted that all of President Obama's interventions "will go with, rather than against, the grain of the market system."

Conservatives may view such assurances with appropriate

skepticism, but it's certainly preferable to hear the president and his associates proclaim their fealty to capitalism rather than declaring that the market system is outmoded or doomed.

BETTER THAN POLAR BEARS

Fortunately, the future of our economic system rests on a firmer foundation than the good faith or competence of passing politicians and government officials, or the puzzling vagaries of public opinion polling. The unprecedented worldwide improvement in living standards in the last century owes everything to the technological innovation, increased productivity, and personal choice that characterize economies driven by competition and the profit motive. Beyond political advances or reverses, beyond the variations in the unemployment figures or the foreclosure rate or the Dow Jones, the fundamental changes in the very terms of human life in the last several generations will help to inspire the sort of confidence (and even gratitude) that will protect the capitalist system from widespread public rejection, destruction, or dismantling.

Consider the direction of the most basic measure of human welfare and opportunity: life expectancy.

Mean life expectancy stood at only thirty years, worldwide, in 1900. This meant that half of all children born in that year would die on or before their thirty-first birthday. By 2008, that number had soared to sixty-five years. In other words, despite the misery and malnutrition and deadly epidemics that afflict the developing world, for all of the 6.5 billion human beings now occupying the planet we have more than doubled the expected span of life.

In the United States, a baby born in 1900 could anticipate forty-seven years of life; by 1950, that number rose to sixty-eight years, and in 2009 it passed a previously unimaginable seventy-eight years.

Put another way, in 1900 American parents with four children (a typical family size at that time) could reasonably expect that at least one of them would die before reaching adulthood. Today, the death of children has, blessedly, become a rarity.

Aside from the figures on health and mortality, consider the difference in the way we live our lives: the opportunity to go on family outings in cars (or airplanes), to enjoy entertainment options inconceivable even to the royalty of the nineteenth century, to attend universities, to speak to loved ones on the other side of the continent, to bathe daily, to retain our teeth through old age, to shop in bookstores stocked more plentifully than the best-equipped libraries of old, to own spacious homes and to tend gardens—all of this makes us easily the most fortunate generation in human history. As former Marxist (and founding father of neoconservatism) Norman Podhoretz summarized recent developments in his latest book, *Why Are Jews Liberals?*: "After World War II, capitalism, instead of collapsing as the socialist faith had led its devotees to expect, began producing wealth on a previously unimaginable scale: not only that, but it made possible a level of prosperity for the poor that surpassed even the rosiest utopian dreams of Marxist theory (or, for that matter, of any other utopian fantasy of the past)." In the United States and around the world, the current economic crisis can neither erase nor obscure the overwhelming and ubiquitous evidence of progress.

I personally savored some of that evidence a few weeks ago

when I attended a dazzling IMAX 3-D documentary of the breathtaking Disney documentary *Earth*. The movie's content left a lasting impression, aside from the technological marvels displayed on the screen and through the sound system. Culled from hours of nature footage previously featured on the BBC and Discovery Channel, *Earth* provided an intimate examination of every sort of living creature in every corner of the planet. The film, narrated by James Earl Jones, strained to provide personality and drama to the experiences of elephants and polar bears and whales and lions and gazelles. The chief revelation of the film, however, involved the common element that linked each of these complex and magnificent creatures: they all spent nearly all their waking hours in efforts to secure the next meal or trying to avoid becoming the next meal for someone else. Their only triumphs and tragedies concerned the basic business of consumption—like the emotional highlight of the film, when a weakened, starving polar bear makes a final effort to attack a robust walrus in the hope of devouring his blubbery flesh and drinking his blood.

For most of man's history, the bulk of humanity lived lives that placed them closer to the food-focused animals than to today's pampered people with our array of choices, joys, adventures, and diversions. Subsistence economies for serfs or peasants or slaves meant that each day represented a struggle to guarantee a meal for self and family. Even in purportedly advanced societies, major portions of the population enjoyed scant time for any activities or initiatives not directly connected to survival.

In 1992, I heard an unforgettable presentation at an Aspen retreat from William Rees-Mogg, distinguished British journalist and onetime editor of the *Times* of London. He recalled his own boyhood in the Depression, when the mass of Britons lived lives only marginally more secure and varied than the struggling polar bears. He estimated the ratio as 80/20 between those who worried and toiled for daily bread while accumulating no wealth and realizing few dreams, with the privileged fifth in the middle class and above with the ability to move up the comfort ladder and provide more for their children. Amazingly, after sixty years, Baron Rees-Mogg estimated that in the United Kingdom the ratio had flipped—with 80 percent now enjoying bourgeois pleasures and opportunities and only 20 percent still desperate and destitute.

He argued that the business system of the west could lead the world to a similar transition, altering the mathematics in which the majority of human beings on the planet still battled for life's basics in 1992.

Amazingly, the last decade and a half brought the realization of his vision, with the overwhelming majority of humankind now beyond the reach of starvation and avoiding that ferocious, animalistic focus on the next meal. That progress came from capitalist economies, or from socialist nations borrowing and adapting the key capitalist tools.

The frustrations and suffering of the last few months must not bring about a total loss of perspective on our situation. The pain of the financial crisis can't overwhelm the obvious fact that we enjoy pleasures and privileges and choices that were all but unthinkable to our own grandparents. Democratic capitalism made that possible, and the proposed dismantling of the business system would threaten to send untold millions back to the sustenance struggles of hungry bears and birds.

"THE GLOBAL CONSENSUS:
REPAIR, NOT REPLACE"

The desire to preserve the foundations of a productive global economy has forged unprecedented international agreement that the current downturn requires adjustments to capitalism but hardly its abandonment. The distinguished French economist Guy Sorman (senior adviser to former prime minister Alain Juppé in the 1990s) acknowledges in his book *Economics Does Not Lie* that "a new kind of financial crisis" demands "new solutions" but adds, "Since the beginning of this crisis, the global consensus among world leaders and economists has been to repair the free-market economy, not to replace it. Some incline to strictly free-market solutions: Let the market clean up the mess and select the winners and the losers. Others prefer state intervention to save financial institutions—but they are not statists, and they do not advocate replacing the free-market economy with a centrally planned one; the state should only act as an insurer of the system. The still-open debate between both schools is not ideological but pragmatic: Which is the quickest way to restart the normal pace of the free economy?"

The outcome of these disputes will help to determine not only the shape of prosperity but the scope of personal liberty. But partisans who misstate the essential nature of the battles that lie ahead will only damage their own effectiveness. We are, at worst, fighting against an unaffordable expansion of government by well-meaning but misguided bureaucrats, not the imposition of socialist tyranny by jackbooted thugs. We're struggling to protect our free-market system from damaging intrusion by

---

NO INNOVATION WITHOUT RISK—
AND BUSINESS CYCLES

Soaring unemployment and ravaged stock prices make it difficult to see benefit from a painful downturn, but economist Guy Sorman maintains that recent reverses should count as a sign of capitalism's health, not its weakness. "Economic cycles are the result of innovation," he writes. "Innovations—whether technical, financial, or managerial—generate growth, but not all innovations are successful. We learn by trial and error, as the economy selects the useful innovations and rejects the useless ones. This process inevitably has its ups and downs. It would be nice to escape economic cycles, but there is no way to have growth without innovation, innovation without risk, or risk without economic cycles. Cycles and downturns are thus not the enemies of economic progress; the enemy of human development is bad economic policies" (*Economics Does Not Lie: A Defense of the Free Market in a Time of Crisis,* 2009).

Washington, not to defend it against definitive obliteration. If President Obama pushes the system the wrong way (and he will), then it is up to conservatives to push back, rather than wringing their hands over the system's imminent destruction.

In fighting for smaller government, we fight for more liberty—not the survival of liberty itself. Yes, that struggle amounts to a "fine old conflict" (which we can ultimately win), but it is by no means The Final Conflict of Communist fantasies and conservative nightmares.

"When the Rich Get Richer,
the Poor Get Poorer"

From the Depths: a view of rich and poor, 1905

"THERE'S NOTHING SURER"

When a dubious economic theory turns up as the punch line in a wildly popular song, it's safe to say that the proposition has deeply penetrated the public's consciousness.

The odd notion that "when the rich get richer, the poor get

poorer" received recognition and publicity in the jaunty foxtrot "Ain't We Got Fun," introduced as part of the vaudeville revue *Satires of 1920* and then recorded by Van & Schenk in a version that became a worldwide hit.

The lyrics, cowritten by Tin Pan Alley legend Gus Kahn, describe a young couple facing hard times.

> *Not much money*
> *Oh but honey*
> *Ain't we got fun!*
> *The rent's unpaid dear*
> *We haven't a bus*
> *But smiles were made dear*
> *For people like us*
>
> *In the winter*
> *In the summer*
> *Don't we have fun?*
> *Times are bum*
> *And getting bummer*
> *Still we have fun*
> *There's nothing surer*
> *The rich get rich*
> *And the poor get . . . children.*

The idea that the rich get richer as the poor get poorer had already established itself as such a cherished cliché by 1920 that the songwriters knew the audience would reach for the familiar word to rhyme with "surer," and they deliver a laugh by mentioning "children" instead. The lyrics go on to describe the arrival of twins for the merry, love-struck couple ("twins and cares dear / come in pairs dear") and then flaunt the "poorer" expectations with a darker edge:

> *Landlords mad and getting madder*
> *Ain't we got fun*
> *Times are bad and getting badder*
> *Still we have fun*
> *There's nothing surer*
> *The rich get rich*
> *And the poor get . . . laid off.*

Though perpetually associated with the flapper era of the 1920s, this little song has never gone out of style, featured in three major movies of the 1950s and turning up as theme music in TV commercials for Carnival Cruise Lines in the 1990s. "Ain't We Got Fun" even drew portentous comment from some of the most significant writers of the twentieth century, including George Orwell (in *The Road to Wigan Pier*), who saw it as a poignant expression of working-class anxiety during the painful recession that followed World War I. Citing the bittersweet lyrics, he noted that "all through the war and for a little time afterwards there had been high wages and abundant employment; things were now returning to something worse than normal, and naturally the working class resisted. The men who had fought had been lured into the army by gaudy promises, and they were coming home to a world where there were no jobs and not even any house. . . . There was a turbulent feeling in the air."

Oddly enough, F. Scott Fitzgerald associated "Ain't We Got Fun" with precisely the same sense of disturbance, change, and menace. In *The Great Gatsby*, the title character shows off his mansion to Daisy Buchanan, his lifelong (and unhappily married) romantic obsession, during a stormy afternoon on Long Island Sound. As his houseguest Klipspringer pounds away at the piano and intones the familiar verses ("In the morning / In the evening/Ain't we got fun"), Daisy and Gatsby share the music, Fitzgerald writes:

"Outside the wind was loud and there was a faint flow of thunder along the Sound. All the lights were going on in West Egg now; the electric trains, men-carrying, were plunging home through the rain from New York. It was the hour of a profound human change, and excitement was generating on the air.

> *'One thing's sure and nothing's surer*
> *The rich get richer and the poor get—children.'* "

The novelist may have misquoted the lyrics (slightly) but he elsewhere echoed their underlying sentiments in his superb 1926 short story "The Rich Boy" (1926), where the narrator begins, "Let me tell you about the very rich. They are different from you and me." Hemingway's famous riposte to this declaration came not in conversation (as an oft-repeated anecdote wrongly suggests) but in his own short story "The Snows of Kilimanjaro," where his protagonist cites "poor Scott Fitzgerald and his romantic awe of them and how he had started a story once that began, 'The very rich are different from you and me.' And how someone had said to Scott, yes, they have more money."

THE RICH AND THE REST OF US

While novelists ruminated on the vast chasm between the rich and the rest of us, activists and radicals dedicated their lives to closing that gap by shattering the power of the "exploiter class." In 1909, the IWW (International Workers of the World, or the Wobblies) proudly published the first edition of the *Little Red Songbook,* with ballads and anthems meant to rally laborers everywhere into "one big union" and to smash capitalism once and for all. The preamble to this collection baldly declared, "The working class and the employing class have nothing in common. Between these two classes a struggle must go on until workers of the world organize as a class, take possession of the earth and the machinery of production, and abolish the wage system." The most famous hymn in the anthology, Ralph Chaplin's "Solidarity Forever," borrowed the melody of "The Battle Hymn of the Republic" to convey its message that the rich built their wealth at the expense of the downtrodden poor:

> *Is there aught we hold in common with the greedy parasite*
> *Who would lash us into serfdom and would crush us with*
>   *his might?*
> *Is there anything left to us but organize and fight?*
> *For the union makes us strong.*
>
> *They have taken untold millions that they never toiled to*
>   *earn*
> *But without our brain and muscle not a single wheel can*
>   *turn*
> *We can break their haughty power, gain our freedom when*
>   *we learn*
> *That the union makes us strong.*

Almost a century later, long after the disintegration of the IWW, even after the collapse of the Soviet Empire and the near universal rejection of Marxist ideas of class struggle, political demagogues and prophets of pop culture continue to peddle the outrageous notion that the creation of wealth by one citizen inevitably leads to the impoverishment of his neighbors.

The 1987 film *Wall Street* (remember, "greed is good") provided memorable expression to the notion that wealthy operators could only enrich themselves by denying benefits to others. Bud Fox, the aspiring trader played by Charlie Sheen, asks his mentor Gordon Gekko (Michael Douglas), "How much is enough?" and the charismatic villain emblematically replies, "It's not a question of enough, pal. It's a zero-sum game, somebody wins, somebody loses. Money itself isn't lost or made, it's simply transferred from one person to another." Later, in one of his windy speeches (as scripted by Oliver Stone), Gekko helpfully explains the basis for economic inequality in America. "The richest one percent of this country owns half our nation's wealth, five trillion dollars," he declares. "One third of that comes from hard work, two thirds comes from inheritance, interest on interest accumulating to widows and idiot sons and what I do, stock and real estate speculation. It's bulls—t. You got ninety percent of the American public out there with little or no net worth. I create nothing. I own. We make the rules, pal. The news, war, peace, famine, upheaval, the price per paper clip. We pick that rabbit out of that hat while everybody else sits out there wondering how the hell we did it. Now you're not naïve enough to think we're living in a democracy, are you buddy? It's the free market."

Inevitably, this old sense of a rigged game—of the arrogant, avaricious few abusing and oppressing the hardworking many—plays a role in our politics and public debates. In his campaign for the presidency in 2000, Vice President Al Gore (the preppy, Harvard-trained son of an influential U.S. senator), framed his struggle as a battle between "the people" and "the powerful." In the next two election cycles (both 2004 and 2008), North Carolina senator John Edwards campaigned for the presidency in a preposterously populist pose. Before the unwelcome focus of attention on his private life, he became famous for an endlessly repeated stump speech that described the nation as painfully and utterly divided. "Today, under George W. Bush, there are two Americas, not one," the blow-dried blowhard, a multimillionaire trial lawyer, solemnly intoned. "One America that does the work, another America that reaps the reward. One America that pays the taxes, another America that gets the tax breaks. One America that will do anything to leave its children a better life, another America that never has to do a thing because its children are already set for life. . . . One America that is struggling to get by, another America that can buy anything it wants, even a Congress and a President" (Des Moines, December 29, 2003). The "two Americas" theme unwittingly conformed to the message of the *Little Red Songbook,* with its emphasis on a "working class" and an "employing class" with "nothing in common."

Senator Edwards's economic and social analysis deserved no more respect and credibility than his marital vows, but countless commentators and candidates promote a similar view of our current economic situation. Lou Dobbs, the carefully coiffed Cassandra of CNN, offered an apocalyptic bestseller in 2006 called *War on the Middle Class.* In its pages, this Harvard-educated resident of a 300-acre horse farm in Sussex County, New Jersey, declares that "ours is becoming increasingly a divided society—a society of haves and have-nots, educated and uneducated, rich and poor. The rich have gotten richer while working people have gotten poorer. . . . What was for almost two hundred years a government of the people has become a government of corporations. . . . In my opinion we are on the verge of not only losing our government of the people, for the people and by the people, but also standing idly by while the American Dream becomes a national nightmare for all of us."

Amusingly, Dobbs attempts to describe an allegedly fresh threat to our age-old Democratic values by recycling familiar class-warfare tropes that would fit just as comfortably into the *Little Red Songbook* of 1909 as they would into antibusiness rants of 1939, 1969, or, for that matter, 2009. In contrasting our present-day "divided society" and "government of corporations" with the previous two hundred years of "government of the people," is he actually suggesting that the poor and middle class enjoyed more prosperity, rights, and opportunities in previous eras of slaveholders, sweat shops, or subsistence farmers?

The laughably ludicrous propositions that elites wielded less power and enjoyed fewer unearned privileges in the eighteenth and nineteenth centuries, and that ordinary working people enjoyed more options and comforts two generations ago (in the depths of the Great Depression), demonstrate the toxic impact of the rich-get-richer/poor-get-poorer lie. The defense and promulgation of that lie require outlandish claims about the levels of suffering and destitution in our peerlessly prosperous society. If the tremendous explosion of American wealth in recent years (slowed but not halted by today's downturn) somehow damaged the prospects and well-being of the nation's poor,

THE ARISTOCRAT WHO FIRST PROMOTED
THE RICHER/POORER LIE

It's ironically appropriate that the first prominent American politician to suggest that the rich get richer when the poor get poorer was also a phony populist who won high office by impersonating a man of the people. In his campaign for the presidency in 1840, General William Henry Harrison, hero of frontier Indian wars and a former U.S. senator, declared, "I believe and I say it is true democratic feeling, that all the measures of government are directed to the purpose of making the rich richer and the poor poorer." His campaign propaganda suggested that the elderly candidate identified as one of the humble folk, and wanted nothing more than to sit in front of his log cabin and drink hard cider; in truth, Harrison grew up on a vast ancestral plantation as the son of Virginia's governor, and his mother traced her descent directly to King Henry III. When the rambunctious "log cabin campaign" brought landslide victory, the new president appeared at his bitterly cold inauguration with no hat, gloves, or overcoat and proceeded to deliver the longest inaugural address in American history (it lasted an excruciating one hour and forty minutes). Shortly thereafter, the sixty-eight-year-old president contracted pneumonia and died in the White House after just thirty days of ignoring issues of rich and poor.

then poverty would be both more prevalent and more abject than in prior decades—a proposition contradicted by all the evidence.

The claim that progress for the rich causes pain for the poor

is logically impossible, historically unsupportable, and cultur-
ally (and psychologically) unforgivable.

DOES WEALTH CAUSE POVERTY?

In his influential and eloquent 1981 bestseller *Wealth and
Poverty,* George Gilder assailed the concept of material well-
being as static and limited. "This mode of thinking, prominent
in foundation-funded reports, best selling economics texts, newspaper columns, and political platforms, is harmless enough on
the surface," he wrote. "But its deeper effect is to challenge the
golden rule of capitalism, to pervert the relation between rich
and poor, and to depict the system as a 'zero-sum game' in
which every gain for someone implies a loss for someone else,
and wealth is seen once again to create poverty."

Historical records from around the world disprove this
cramped and pessimistic point of view. Whenever a nation's
business leadership achieves conspicuous success in building
dynamic companies and accumulating wealth (as in Italy in the
1400s, Holland in the 1600s, Britain in the nineteenth century,
the United States in the last hundred years, or China and India
since 1990), the poor in those countries don't suffer; they benefit with the rest of the population. But beyond the abundance of
international examples, there's the simpler perspective of personal experience and common sense.

In 1996, my wife and I moved with our three children to
Seattle and, like most denizens of the Great Northwet, we took
immediate pride in the world-famous plutocrats who became
our new neighbors. Thanks to spectacular success in the software and cell phone businesses, for a time the much-publicized

list of the nation's wealthiest individuals showed four out of the top ten living in the Seattle area. In all the years we've raised our family in western Washington, we've never once heard a local resident express resentment over the fact that some of the richest people on the planet choose to live in our region. In fact, tour operators who take tens of thousands of visitors on boat trips on Lake Washington feature glimpses of the sprawling Gates mansion as a point of local pride. People might criticize Bill Gates for his public pronouncements, or register their complaints about the products he and his team unleash from Microsoft, but none of these skeptics ever expresses the wish that the billionaire would pack up his family and move to L.A. or London.

The presence of unimaginably wealthy people enriches our area in both tangible and intangible terms. It's not just the obvious addition to the tax base, or the lavish level of charitable giving—with local museums, parklands, performing-arts institutions, universities, sports stadiums, and much more benefiting handsomely from the generosity of the Gates family and his idiosyncratic Microsoft cofounder, Paul Allen. There's also an energy, a cosmopolitan atmosphere, and a sense of world-class swagger that comes to any community able to spawn and retain some of the most productive and powerful entrepreneurs in existence. Far from swallowing up limited resources that would otherwise nourish the middle class and the poor, a city's most successful businessmen generate and contribute resources that benefit everyone. States that impose punishing tax rates that chase away their richest residents and most dynamic businesses do nothing to improve the lot of the less fortunate.

A major study for the American Legislative Exchange Council published in March 2009 analyzed demographic records from 1998 to 2007—a period in which 1,100 people every day (including weekends and holidays) moved from the nine states with the highest income tax (California, New Jersey, New York, Ohio, and others) and relocated, primarily to the nine states with *no* state income tax (including Florida, Nevada, New Hampshire, Texas, and Tennessee). During those same years, states with no income tax created 89 percent more jobs and provided a 32 percent faster growth in personal income than their tax-to-the-max counterparts. In 2008, a single state with no income tax—Texas—created more new jobs than all forty-nine other states combined. Economists Arthur Laffer and Stephen Moore point out the insurmountable problem for "states that want to pry more money out of the wallets of rich people. It never works because people, investment capital and businesses are mobile. They can leave tax-unfriendly states and move to tax friendly states." This represents a particular problem for painfully broke California, where the continual arrival of hordes of impoverished immigrants (legal and illegal) can't effectively replace the established entrepreneurs and wage earners who regularly depart for regions with a more favorable business climate. In a state of 38 million people, the top 1 percent of those who pay income tax—a mere 144,000 successful individuals and households—provide more than 50 percent of the total tax revenue. This means that the departure of even a few hundred of these crucial burden-bearers amounts to a disaster for a struggling state. They've been leaving each year by the thousands.

Here in Seattle, the 2001 decision by Boeing to move its corporate headquarters to Chicago (with special tax incentives and concessions from the pliant Illinois legislature) struck all segments of the populace as a disaster. The big aircraft company

"SHARE OUR WEALTH"

No politician exploited the divisions between rich and poor more radically or profitably than Louisiana governor and U.S. senator Huey P. Long, the Depression-era demagogue universally known as "The Kingfish." Beginning in 1933, he organized the national Share Our Wealth Society to promote sweeping redistribution of the nation's economic resources. Within two years, his operation (organized by Gerald L.K. Smith, later notorious as the white-supremacist, anti-Semitic leader of America's pro-Hitler "Silver Shirts") boasted 7.5 million members organized in 27,000 clubs in every corner of the country. This popular mass movement focused on the concentration of great riches in the hands of bankers and manufacturers, suggesting that the nation produced enough wealth for every individual to live comfortably were the money divided more equitably. Long wrote a catchy song called "Every Man a King" to rally support for his program:

> *Why weep or slumber America*
> *Land of brave and true*
> *With castles and clothing and food for all*
> *All belongs to you!*
> *Ev'ry man a King, ev'ry man a King*
> *For you can be a millionaire*
> *But there's something belonging to others*
> *There's enough for all people to share.*

The song became a national sensation, as performed by the well-known band Ina Ray Hutton and her all-girl orchestra, the Melodears.

On the Senate floor and in frequent radio addresses, Long promised to provide a "household estate" of $5,000 (almost $80,000 in today's dollars) for every struggling family, while guaranteeing an annual income of $2,500 ($40,000 today). To pay for this largesse, incomes above $1 million would be taxed at a rate of 100 percent, and all personal wealth in excess of $8 million would be confiscated for redistribution. "Let no one tell you that it is difficult to redistribute the wealth of this land," he told a 1934 radio audience. "It is simple." When critics accused Long of Marxist tendencies, he responded indignantly, "Communism? Hell No! This plan is the only defense this country's got *against* communism." He planned to use the spreading Share Our Wealth movement to create a third-party presidential campaign to challenge FDR in 1936, but an assassin shot him at close range in the lavish state capitol building in Baton Rouge that Long himself had built. The Kingfish was only forty-two.

reassured Washingtonians that they had no plans to close down their major manufacturing facilities in our area, or to end their century-long association with the region, and that the strategic shift to the Midwest would cost only 500 executive jobs. Nevertheless, everyone from Governor Gary Locke (now secretary of commerce in the Obama administration) to cabdrivers on the scenic streets of Seattle understood that the departure of top brass from an international corporation darkened the future for the area's overall economy.

Governments and chambers of commerce aren't crazy when they fight ferociously to keep prospering businesses where they are, or to lure new companies from other states. Under the logic of the-rich-get-richer/the-poor-get-poorer, they should welcome plans by any local enterprise to relocate, because that will leave behind more "wealth" for the working class. Fortunately, most people understand that if a corporation moves away, it means fewer jobs and less productive activity in the local economy. It doesn't take some leap of comprehension and logic to then reach the obvious conclusion that it's also a blow if the business leaders who provide the jobs and generate productive activity decide to pursue profit somewhere else.

"THERE GOES THE NEIGHBORHOOD"

If a prominent corporate executive decides to buy a new home on your block, there's little chance you'll hear the comment "There goes the neighborhood." The addition of a few well-off neighbors can raise property values and prestige for everyone else. When the guy next door begins making more money and goes through a major remodeling or stylish landscaping or even adds a second story, as long as he doesn't block your view, it's reason for celebration, not resentment. When the prospering folks across the street get a new roof or a fresh paint job or decide to install a swimming pool, they've done nothing to damage your enjoyment of your own home. They may inspire other householders in the area to make their own improvements, and at the very worst, they've provided well-paid employment for contractors, gardeners, architects. An increase in wealth for one family never causes an increase in poverty for others on the block or, for that matter, takes resources away from strangers on the other side of town.

If, on the other hand, an impoverished family occupies the house a few doors away, it's only natural to worry about the future stability of the neighborhood. On occasion, such responses stem from racial prejudice—which is both irrational and indecent. In many instances, however, it makes sense to feel concerned about a sudden influx of poor people into the immediate vicinity. The well-established, longtime residents might reasonably worry that a big wave of fresh arrivals could depress home prices, or place major demands on the community without bringing the new resources to help fulfill them. In this situation, the newcomers may ultimately surprise old-timers with their unexpected energy, family values, or hard work, but it's still rare to hear any homeowner welcome poor neighbors with the assumption that they'll make him look and feel rich by comparison. No one wants to see a home on his block become overcrowded and run-down, with peeling paint, unkempt yards, and junked cars on cinderblocks on the front lawn just so he now can claim to own the nicest house on the street. The dramatic changes in both deteriorating and gentrifying districts show that even nonrelated families generally rise or fall together, seeing whole neighborhoods improve or decline. New wealth brings more wealth, just as deepening poverty leads to more poverty. And increased riches for some don't lead to deprivation for others, any more than impoverishment for some guarantees enhanced wealth for others.

Long before the free-market theories of Milton Friedman,

George Gilder, Thomas Sowell, or even Adam Smith, a celebrated British clergyman named Thomas Fuller (1608–61) understood the basic principle that individual advancement depended on the success, not the failure, of your fellow citizens. He wrote, "Let him who expects one class of society to prosper in the highest degree, while the other is in distress, try whether one side of the face can smile while the other is pinched."

"THE POOR LIVE MOSTLY ON THE RICH"

This economic interdependence becomes even more obvious in the workplace than in residential districts. "Bosses" and "workers," the allegedly opposing castes endlessly invoked by class-struggle rabble-rousers, actually depend on the success of precisely the same companies. In the fierce competition of free markets, bosses gain nothing if a seething workforce feels short-changed and exploited, and the employees earn no long-term benefit if the company they serve starts losing money. It's true that increased revenue won't necessarily bring higher wages (since a shortsighted boss might choose maximizing profits over improving living standards), but business success certainly increases the likelihood of better salaries and bonuses. With all the fervent hostility of the smash-capitalism agitators of the last century, no theorist has been able to explain how harming your own employer or striking blows against the economic system in general will help you bring home a bigger paycheck or contribute to keeping your job secure.

The baleful experience of General Motors, once counted among the most dynamic and powerful of all U.S. corporations, provides an instructive example. For several decades, the United

Auto Workers secured contracts that meant that workers gained more steadily than the company that wrote their checks, but this imbalance brought an implacable reckoning. After the government bailout (or takeover, to use the less delicate phrase), no one can mistake the reality that workers and bosses (and federal administrators) will either fail together or succeed together, especially since the union now owns the biggest share of the company. Even before bankruptcy and restructuring, it should have been obvious that employees would suffer if their company suffered, and would gain if their corporation gained. Any worker in any field who believes that he'll benefit if the boss suffers business reverses is, quite simply, too stupid for continued employment.

If the logic of interdependence applies in the workplace and on a local and regional basis, it operates even more decisively on the national level. If the "rich get richer" in the Indian high-tech center of Bangalore, it hardly means that the "poor get poorer" elsewhere on the Deccan Plateau. The new prosperity for the best-trained and most industrious citizens of the world's largest democracy may not bring instant relief to India's impoverished hordes, but it definitely opens new opportunities for many of them and feeds an unprecedented expansion of the middle class. Naturally, economic planners on the subcontinent would prefer that their homegrown talent pursue careers in India rather than migrating to American companies in Silicon Valley or Redmond, Washington. Rich people—even the "idle rich" of socialist fantasies, with their inherited millions—add to a national economy through investment and production and consumption, rather than subtracting from it by exhausting some fixed supply of assets.

When my late father decided to make his life in Israel at age sixty-four, he did no damage to native-born Israelis by taking up limited space or resources in an already crowded country. Even though he arrived without significant capital and at a relatively advanced age, he brought his vision and energy and indomitable optimism and soon launched a business that created scores of high-tech jobs. Though he never became rich, he did grow richer—a process that obviously did nothing to impoverish his new homeland. Israel has become the most successful economy in the Middle East by welcoming literally millions of such immigrants (particularly from ancient Jewish communities in the Islamic world and from the former Soviet Union), whose economic progress raised living standards and competitiveness for the whole population, even longtime residents.

For the global economy, prosperity for one nation doesn't mean hardship or oppression for another. In the last thirty years, more than 80 percent of all the world's economies experienced unprecedented and simultaneous growth (with the notable exception of some of the failed states of sub-Saharan Africa). If Mexico enjoys boom years, that hardly hurts the United States. Economic dynamism south of the border not only generates a more eager market for U.S. exports but also slows the flow of desperate immigrants, who then undercut the wages of native-born Americans. The spectacular development of China not only adds purchasing power to the world's most populous nation for the import of selected U.S. goods and media but also creates more capital to lend to the cash-strapped American government. When investors wake up in the predawn hours to check the progress of the Tokyo Stock Exchange, they're not rooting for falling prices. If Chile produces a bumper crop of plums, that doesn't mean a shortage of plums in California; at worst, it might result in more and better fruit, at lower prices.

The remarkable advances in instant communication and long-distance transportation make interdependence inevitable, even across international boundaries.

Ambrose Bierce, columnist, curmudgeon, poet, Civil War hero and author of the savagely insightful *The Devil's Dictionary,* unforgettably lampooned the share-the-wealth, limited-resources demagoguery of the redistributionists of his era. Shortly before his mysterious disappearance while riding with Mexican revolutionary Pancho Villa in 1913, Bierce wrote a remarkably prescient treatise called "The Socialist—What He Is, and Why."

"His unreason is what he is a socialist with," Bierce sneered. "The socialist notion appears to be that the world's wealth is a fixed quantity, and A can acquire only by depriving B. He is fond of figuring the rich as living upon the poor—riding on their backs." But even a hundred years ago, "Bitter Bierce" (as his many critics derided him) understood that economic progress for one segment of society benefited every segment of society. "The plain truth of the matter is that the poor live mostly on the rich. . . . A man may remain in poverty all his life and be not only of no advantage to his fellow poor men, but by his competition in the labor market a harm to them; for in the abundance of labor lies the cause of low wages, as even a socialist knows. As a consumer the man counts for little, for he consumes only the bare necessaries of life. But, if he pass from poverty to wealth he not only ceases to be a competing laborer; he becomes a consumer of everything that he used to want—all the luxuries by production of which nine-tenths of the labor class live he now buys. He has added his voice to the chorus of demand. . . . All the industries of the world are so interrelated and interdependent that none is unaffected in some infinitesimal degree by the new stimulation."

THE INFAMOUS INCOME GAP VERSUS PROGRESS FOR THE POOR

Unable to muster any sort of logical support for their attempt to associate soaring prosperity for the most fortunate with deepening poverty for the least fortunate, inequality obsessives resort to the manipulation of data and history. While no study in the last twenty years shows the poor actually "getting poorer" in terms of accepted measures of living standards, there is abundant indication of a growing wealth gap between those at the very top and the bottom of the income scale. As the rich get richer, the poor also get richer—dramatically richer—but redistributionists express horror at the fact that the distance between the least and most successful continues to increase.

In a typical jeremiad from the Age of Reagan (September 7, 1986), Barbara Ehrenreich posed a painful question in the *New York Times Magazine* under the headline "Is the Middle Class Doomed?" She reported that "some economists have predicted that the middle class will disappear altogether, leaving the country torn, like many third world countries, between an affluent minority and throngs of the desperately poor." Some twenty years later, Lou Dobbs made a strikingly similar prediction in his book *War on the Middle Class,* suggesting that doom was in fact on hand for the Great American Bourgeoisie: "Our political, business, and academic elites are waging an outright war on Americans, and I doubt the middle class can survive the continued assault by forces unleashed over the past five years if they go on unchecked."

As Arthur Laffer, Stephen Moore, and Peter Tanous make clear in their hugely important book *The End of Prosperity* (2008), reports of middle-class doom and demise have been greatly exaggerated. "Here's the truth," they write. "The purchasing power of the median income family, that is, families at the midpoint of the income continuum, rose to $54,061 in 2004, an $8,228 real increase since 1980. The middle class is not disappearing . . . it is getting richer."

In fact, the entire nation has gotten richer, very much including the poor. America's net worth increased in real, constant dollar terms from $25 trillion in 1980 to $57 trillion in 2007. As Laffer, Moore, and Tanous note, "More wealth was created in the United States over the past twenty-five years than in the previous two hundred years. . . . In 1967 only one in 25 families earned an income of $100,000 or more in real income (in 2004 dollars), whereas now, almost one in four families do."

The "rising income gap" actually reflects increased wealth for the most prosperous rather than falling living standards for the poor, and even so, this famous gap represents something of a statistical anomaly. A recent study by the Congressional Budget Office (May 2007) showed that from 1994 to 2004, of all Americans, the poorest enjoyed the highest percentage increase in their incomes. In other words, far from being left behind, the least-privileged Americans are making faster progress than any other segment of the population. A subsequent report by the Treasury Department ("Income Mobility in the U.S. from 1996 to 2005"; November 13, 2007) reached the same conclusions, with those in the bottom 20 percent of wage earners improving their median income by a breathtaking 109 percent (inflation-adjusted). By comparison, the top quintile raised its median income by a relatively modest 8.7 percent. The Treasury report (examining returns for a huge sample of 168,300 taxpayers) concluded, "Economic growth resulted in rising incomes for most taxpayers over the period of 1996 to 2005 . . . the real incomes of two-thirds of all taxpayers increased over this period. Further, the median income of those initially in the lower income groups increased more than the median incomes of those in the higher income groups." The Nobel Prize–winning economic historian Robert Fogel observed in 2004, "In every measure that we have bearing on the standard of living . . . the gains of the lower classes have been far greater than those experienced by the population of a whole."

With this sort of encouraging progress for the least prosperous Americans, how could the wealth gap possibly increase? The answer involves a statistical anomaly, and the contradiction between government figures measuring income rise in percentage terms and numbers that report the rich-and-poor gap in raw dollars.

Imagine two citizens, the well-to-do Smith and the struggling Jones. Smith earns $200,000 a year and increases his income by an impressive 10 percent. Jones, on the other hand, brings home only $20,000 a year but succeeds in raising his earnings by a spectacular 20 percent. That means Jones receives $24,000 the next year, while Smith gets $220,000.

In other words, even though the poor, hardworking Jones has lifted his earnings twice as fast as the wealthy Smith, the income gap between them has still increased—from $180,000 to $196,000. Because Jones starts from a much lower base income, even a far more rapid improvement can't stop the expansion of the overall earnings differential.

DEFENDING "THE DECADE OF GREED"

No era in American history became more prominently associated with the chasm between rich and poor than Ronald Reagan's 1980s—frequently called "The Me Decade" or "The Decade of Greed." The hit television shows *Dallas* and *Dynasty* caricatured the recklessness and ruthlessness of wealthy, glamorous, and amorous families, while Tom Wolfe's epic novel *The Bonfire of the Vanities* focused on the corrupt and vacuous lives of Wall Street "Masters of the Universe." It's certainly true that the rich got richer during the decade—but so did the poor and nearly everyone else. The unemployment rate plummeted from just under 10 percent in 1981 to below 6 percent at the end of the 1980s. The median income increased by 10 percent between 1982 and 1988, and income for the lowest-earning 20 percent rose nearly 13 percent.

Meanwhile, the wealthy paid a higher—not lower—share of the total income tax burden, because of President Reagan's tax cuts. As Dinesh D'Souza pointed out in *Forbes* magazine ("The Decade of Greed That Wasn't," November 3, 1997), "The affluent paid more in federal taxes than ever before. Even though the top marginal rate declined from 70 percent to 28 percent, the proportion of taxes collected from the top 1 percent of income earners went from 18 percent of all revenues in 1981 to 28 percent in 1988. The top 5 percent of earners bore 35 percent of the tax burden in 1981. In 1988, Reagan's last year in office, they paid 46 percent. Meanwhile, the tax share of middle- and lower-income Americans declined." The lower rates brought increased economic activity and more revenue, in part by reducing the desire for elaborate tax-avoidance strategies.

Contrary to the image of selfishness and greed perpetuated by the media, D'Souza points out, "The well-off not only paid more in taxes but also gave more in charity. The Reagan era saw the greatest outpouring of private generosity in history. Americans, who contributed around $65 billion (as measured in 1990 dollars) to charity in 1980 gave more than $100 billion annually by the end of the decade, a real increase of 54 percent." Economist Richard McKenzie calculated that the increase in charitable contributions was greater than in any previous time of the postwar era, and that the growth of charitable giving easily exceeded the increase in luxury expenditures like jewelry, restaurants, and health club memberships.

By focusing almost exclusively on the disparity between those who earn most and those who earn least, rather than reporting on the remarkable progress in income and living standards for even the poorest among us, major media distort and exaggerate the problems of poverty and inequality. David R. Henderson of the Hoover Institution at Stanford University suggests that "because of the problems with measuring income and adjusting for inflation, there's a better way to measure the wellbeing of a household: see what's in the house."

Robert Rector of the Heritage Foundation did just that in an important paper in August 2007, using detailed and authoritative government figures. According to this research, among the

37 million Americans officially classified as living below the poverty line, 97 percent own color televisions, more than 50 percent own two or more color TVs, 78 percent have a VCR or a DVD player, and 62 percent receive cable or satellite TV reception. Eighty percent of poor households boast air-conditioning, 89 percent have microwave ovens, and nearly three-quarters own a car. An impressive 31 percent have two or more cars.

TODAY'S POOR BEAT YESTERDAY'S MIDDLE CLASS

Most surprisingly, 43 percent of all poor households actually own their own homes, and the average home owned by households classified as poor by the Census Bureau is a three-bedroom house with one and a half baths, a garage, and a porch or patio. Even considering poor people who rent apartments, or live with extended family, the average poor American enjoys more living space than the average middle-class individual in Paris, London, Vienna, Athens, and other European cities.

The old stereotype of poor kids going hungry no longer applies to the United States. As Rector reports, "The average consumption of protein, vitamins, and minerals is virtually the same for poor and middle-class children and, in most cases, is well above recommended norms. . . . Eighty-nine percent of the poor report their families have 'enough' food to eat, while only 2 percent say they 'often' don't get enough to eat."

The numbers show that today's poor not only enjoy a vastly better living standard than the poor of previous generations, they actually enjoy more comfortable lives than the middle class of some thirty years ago. The Federal Reserve of Dallas used Census Bureau numbers to compare poor households in 2005 with "all households" in 1970, and the poor households of today are more likely to own washing machines, clothes dryers, dishwashers, refrigerators, stoves, color TVs, telephones, and air conditioners—not to mention recently invented conveniences like DVD players and cell phones. In other words, by simple, homey measures of comfort and convenience, the lowest rung on the income ladder lives better lives today than average middle-class Americans of the last generation. More significant measures show similarly substantial expansions in opportunities for struggling families: while children of poor households face far more challenges in attending college than children of affluent parents, they still manage to do so in greater numbers and percentages than typical middle-class Americans of thirty years ago.

What makes these achievements particularly impressive is the high percentage of the nation's poor who constitute new arrivals to this country. According to Census Bureau figures, a full one-quarter of all poor persons in the United States are now immigrants or the first-generation minor children of those immigrants. Approximately one in ten among the poor (or nearly four million individuals) is either an illegal immigrant or the under-eighteen child of that illegal.

Nothing more dramatically illustrates the prodigious ability of the U.S. economy to generate and spread wealth than the rewards and opportunities earned by those classified as poor—especially when such a substantial proportion of those in that category entered the nation recently, and often without authorization.

NO PERMANENTLY SEPARATE
AND UNEQUAL CAMPS

The term *poor* hardly counts as a permanent designation, like *female* or *Native American*. For most people it represents a temporary phase of life rather than a final destination. The more than forty million legal and illegal immigrants (the majority of whom do *not* live below the poverty line) highlight the problem with the tired old poor-get-poorer mantra. Many immigrants may come to America poor, but they don't remain destitute forever. The rise of most immigrants is obvious, predictable, and impressive: if they secure jobs and homes, learn the language, and acculturate to a new society, they will generally begin the process of earning, saving, and advancement made famous by previous generations of migrants. That advancement becomes especially notable with American-raised children of parents born abroad—like a young doctor of my acquaintance, who grew up as the daughter of a cleaning lady from El Salvador and ultimately won a scholarship to UCLA Medical School.

For native-born and immigrants alike, escape from poverty isn't just possible, it's probable. Research from the Federal Reserve, the U.S. Census Bureau, and the Treasury Department tell the same story: among those in the bottom 20 percent in household income, a full fifth will move to a higher quintile within a single year, and the majority will move up within a decade. After twenty years, a poor family is as likely to bring home enough income to qualify for one of the top two quintiles (the leading 40 percent of earners) as that family is to remain at the bottom of the income ladder.

The key element in this persistent and widespread mobility is the acquisition of new skills and work experience, strongly correlated with age. Young people are disproportionately poor, reflecting the fact that most of us begin our work lives at the bottom of the pay scale. At my first full-time job (at age seventeen, during sophomore year of college) I earned minimum wage, and my wife (who went on to earn her PhD in psychology) got similar payment for her service as a part-time telephone operator. Most people take such jobs early in their lives but quickly move upward and onward, or at least receive raises and promotions in the places where they started.

In identifying the composition of the least privileged segment of the economy, David R. Henderson writes, "The most important factor is age. Heavily represented in the bottom quintile are young people who have just graduated from high school or college and are living on their own. Their current earnings are low, but as they age and gain skills, their earnings rise. Similarly, overrepresented in the lowest quintile are retired people who may be wealthier than the average family but don't have high incomes. Other factors matter, too. A worker who has lost a job may have had a low annual income one year, but then he finds another job. Or a divorced mother may be in the lowest quintile, but nine years later she is remarried or working in a productive job and has a much higher family income."

In a brilliant paper for the Center of the American Experiment, John Hinderaker and Scott W. Johnson delineated "The Truth About Income Inequality" and concluded that the data show "that much of what passes for inequality between rich and poor is really inequality between generations. America is not a country in the process of stratifying into permanently separate and unequal camps, one rich and one poor. Rather, it is a country that offers its young people and immigrants unprecedented opportunity to achieve financial success.

"If the rich person and poor person are, in large part, the same person at different stages of life, it is reasonable to ask if there is anything objectionable about the 'inequality' that results from the fact that a mature, experienced, established worker can earn more money than one who, in the early stages of his career, lacks those advantages. It appears clear that far from being objectionable, this type of 'inequality' is an inherent and desirable characteristic of an advanced society."

Hinderaker and Johnson also make the brilliant point that the different rewards that go to various components of society aren't assigned by some allotment committee or given out according to bureaucratic policy. "Discussions of income distribution are inherently misleading in one fundamental respect," they write. "Income is not distributed. It is earned. This fact, while obvious, is often overlooked."

NO IMMUTABLE DIVISIONS

The United States has been uniquely blessed with the understanding that the designations *rich* and *poor* denote transient status, not caste. In the rest of the world, the belief that the wealthy and the impoverished remain divided by an immutable, unbridgeable gap produces not only personal despair and resentment but also social instability and oppression. Tyrants always emphasize enduring class distinctions, together with the claim that only their own limitless power can transcend them. "Mankind is divided into rich and poor, into property owners and exploited and to abstract oneself from this fundamental division; and from the antagonism between poor and rich, means abstracting oneself from fundamental facts," wrote Joseph Stalin in 1937. In the years that followed, his murder of millions demonstrated that distinctions between powerful and powerless, between master and slave, count as far more "fundamental," painful, and ultimately deadly than divisions between rich and poor.

DAMAGING OTHERS BY EARNING MORE?

This insight puts the proper perspective on the common complaints about the "unfair" distribution of income and the demand that our political leaders do something to correct it. This pressure seems to presume that all income flows to some centralized authority, where all-powerful potentates decide precisely how they should hand it out. Even in the Obama Era, with the federal government ambitiously assuming a broad array of unprecedented functions, there's been no effort (so far) to establish a Department of Income Allocation. As William L. Anderson of the Ludwig von Mises Institute writes in "The Income Inequality Hoax," "Income is not something that just randomly flows into an economy. It is the result of individuals providing productive services that are purchased in a marketplace."

If someone takes home more than his neighbor, it's not because he's exerted more influence on the powerful people who dispense society's goodies to one and all, but because his employer has freely agreed to higher payment for the services that the fortunate earner has freely agreed to perform.

Yet even if there's nothing inherently unjust about different people earning very different salaries for the very different work they perform, many social critics worry about the wounding psychological impact of income inequality. An individual may feel small, frustrated, vulnerable, and ashamed if he's regularly reminded that he makes vastly less than other people at the same company or in the same neighborhood. According to this argument, self-esteem may suffer an even more substantial blow if the struggling worker believes his own low salary is justified.

An extreme example of such logic came in a bizarre 2005 international bestseller by Richard Layard, a member of the British House of Lords. In *Happiness: Lessons from a New Science,* Lord Layard draws some spectacularly unscientific conclusions. "Over the last 50 years, we in the west have enjoyed unparalleled economic growth," he allows. "We have better homes, cars, holidays, jobs, education, and above all, health. But are we happier? Not in the least, and this worried me. Economics is all to do with growth and national prosperity. But what's the point of more cash in the pockets if people are more miserable?"

Because he concludes that hard work poisons an individual's quality of life and provokes resentment from the people around him, Lord Layard recommends punitive taxes like those we use to decrease consumption of tobacco. "If we make taxes commensurate to the damage that an individual does to others when he earns more, then he will only work harder if there is a true net benefit to society as a whole. It is efficient to discourage work effort that makes society worse off," he writes.

Arthur Brooks of the American Enterprise Institute scoffs at the notion of a special tax to suppress hard work and productivity and notes the utter lack of evidence that income disparities produce unhappiness or self-pity. As he writes in the *Wall Street*

Journal (July 19, 2007), "The evidence reveals that it is not economic inequality that frustrates Americans. It is a perceived lack of opportunity. To focus our policies on inequality, instead of opportunity, is to make a serious error—one that will worsen the very problem that we seek to solve and make us generally unhappier."

In his book *Gross National Happiness,* Brooks tartly observes that "policymakers and economists rarely denounce the scandal of inequality in work effort, creativity, talent, or enthusiasm. We almost never hear about the outrage that is America's inequality in time with friends, love, faith, or fun—even though these are things most of us care about more than we do money. . . . To believe that we truly redress inequality in our society by moving cash around is to take a materialistic—and totally unrealistic—view of life. To focus on income redistribution is to profess a mechanistic and impoverished understanding of the resources Americans truly value."

The focus on wealth discrepancies not only diminishes our view of the freakishly fortunate society in which we live but also poisons our own ability to enjoy our personal blessings. Your pride and satisfaction with the beautiful home you've built will wither if you cast jealous eyes on the even larger and more stylish house that your neighbor has redecorated up the block. The romantic relationship with your own beautiful and brilliant wife will grow stale and sour if you obsess on the even sexier, more desirable mate who goes to bed every night with your best friend. And your excitement about a raise and promotion will feel short-lived and meaningless if you can't stop thinking about the undeserving and terminally lazy lunkhead who took over the corner office with the spectacular view and earns far more than you clawed your way to achieve.

"ENGINEERING EQUALITY"

A team of economists led by Robert Shiller of Yale recently developed a scheme to limit the gap between rich and poor. The so-called Rising-Tide Tax System based its title on John F. Kennedy's celebrated aphorism that a "rising tide lifts all boats," and adopted this idea to ensure that a rising tide would lift top tax rates. The proposal would require that tax brackets go through an automatic recalibration at the end of every year, based on any changes in the share of total national income earned by each income category. In other words, if the top fifth of wage earners saw their share of national income rise, then their tax rates would rise correspondingly the next year, to provide more money for the families whose share of overall income had declined. According to the designers of the novel mechanism, this would effectively freeze everyone's share of after-tax income at the same constant level, with no more chance that the rich get richer while the poor get poorer. As Stephen Mihm glowingly reported in the *New York Times Magazine* (December 14, 2008), "The proposal is progressive in intent but conservative in effect. The only 'redistribution' it promises would be an automatic response to growing inequality." Professor Shiller claims that this automatic governmental recalculation of economic rewards would benefit "all members of society." He confidently declares, "It's something we can engineer."

The problem, of course, is the assumption that when the top-income Americans earn ever-increasing shares of national income, it's just an accidental or arbitrary phenomenon, rather than a reflection of harder work and enhanced productivity by the most industrious and creative people in the society. These leading earners drive the periods of growth that bring wage increases and improved living standards across the board. They already pay more taxes for every extra dollar they bring home, so it makes little sense to punish their additional toil and success with higher rates. Smug academics and journalists may revel in their presumed ability to engineer equality but with this scheme they would succeed only in engineering injustice and undermining prosperity.

"DON'T ENVY YOUR BUDDY HIS COW"

Dwelling on the privileges and triumphs of others rather than emphasizing your own achievements not only provides a reliable road to failure and misery but also violates an essential element of Western morality. In giving human beings the Ten Commandments, God offers a series of orders regarding our obligations to Him and our behavior to others, but only one of the directives centers on our emotions. The climactic Tenth Commandment strictly forbids diminishing our own success by measuring it against the accomplishments of others: "You shall not covet your neighbor's house. You shall not covet your neighbor's wife, his manservant, his maidservant, his ox, his donkey, nor anything that belongs to your neighbor."

In a simultaneously hilarious and profound presentation to the Cato Institute in the nation's capital (August 1997), humorist and economics guru P.J. O'Rourke asked the big question about the Tenth Commandment: "I mean, here are God's basic rules for how we should live, a very brief list of sacred obligations and solemn moral precepts, and right at the end of it is: 'Don't envy your buddy his cow.' What is that doing there? Why would God, with just 10 things to tell Moses, choose jealousy about the stuff the guy next door has? Well, think about how important to the well-being of a community that commandment actually is. What that commandment says is that if you want a donkey, if you want a pot roast, if you want a cleaning lady, don't bitch about it, go get your own!"

O'Rourke memorably and passionately targeted the folly involved with those who yearn to close the "wealth gap." He explained that "the world doesn't need to be thinking about the wealth gap; the world needs to be thinking about wealth. Wealth is good. Everybody knows that about his own wealth. Wealth improves your life; it improves your family's life. You invest in wise and worthwhile things, and you help your friends and neighbors. Your life would get better if you got rich, and the lives of all the people around you would get better if you got rich. Your wealth is good. So why isn't everybody else's wealth good, too? I don't get it."

LOWERING ALL BOATS

O'Rourke's point (and God's) involves the importance of economic interdependence—the idea that we all benefit from one another's successes and suffer from one another's disasters—and understanding that serves as the glue holding together a family, a community, or a society. Recognition of this connectedness strengthens bonds of fellowship, just as surely as the "rich-get-richer-when-the-poor-get-poorer" belief serves to weaken them. As Hinderaker and Johnson conclude from their exhaustive research, "Americans in all income groups have prospered, or have failed to prosper, together. Gains by upper-income Americans have not come at the expense of middle- or lower-income Americans. Nor has anyone else gained in those periods when higher-income families have lost ground."

One of the few unexpected benefits of the current economic crisis involves a reminder of the timeless truth and relevance of that essential message. Since the recession intensified in 2008, higher-income families have certainly lost ground and no American has benefited from their misfortune. In our present predicament, the poor may well have gotten poorer, but the rich have gotten *much* poorer—losing an estimated average of 40 percent of net worth. Working people have faced painful cuts in salary and benefits, but the vertigo-inducing decline of real estate, stocks, and other investments made well-to-do families (and not just Madoff investors) the most visible and often most desperate victims of the downturn.

In 2008, an astonishing 2.5 million households lost their status as "millionaires"—an unprecedented decline of 38 percent in the number of families with net worth of at least a million dollars, excluding primary residence. This followed unparalleled growth in the millionaires' club, with its inflation-adjusted membership more than quadrupling (to 9.2 million) in the seven brief years from 2001 to 2007.

Skeptics have always questioned John F. Kennedy's aphorism about a rising tide lifting all boats. Liberal economist (and Bill Clinton adviser) Gene Sperling, for instance, commented that without protective policies from an activist government, "the rising tide will lift some boats, but others will run aground." Even those who doubt the positive impact of wealth creation among society's most productive and privileged can now see the negative results of shrinking assets at the top of the economic pyramid. While we can debate the potential influence of some future rising tide, it's obvious that the steadily receding tide has left no one happily afloat or cruising confidently toward safe harbor.

"THE IMPENDING RICH"

It's a perfect moment, in fact ("in the meantime/in between time"), to return to the infectious irony of "Ain't We Got Fun"— with its message of savoring romance and merriment despite economic hardship. The song has lasted as long as it has because it conveys no hint of class envy or anger at the rich—the lyrics make no wistful references to the Rockefellers or their fellow plutocrats, as did other ditties of that early jazz-age era.

The words, after all, make the same point that Arthur Brooks emphasizes in his study of happinesss—that factors besides money play the greatest role in our contentment. In that context, the suggestion that

> —there's nothing surer
> The rich get rich and the poor get . . . children

may not seem like an entirely bad deal. After all, the loving couple gets generous consolation for their apparent (and probably temporary) poverty:

> Just to make their trouble
> Nearly double

Something happened last night
To their chimney a gray bird came
Mister Stork is his name
And I'll bet two pins
A pair of twins
Just happen'd in with the bird
Still they're very gay and merry
Just at dawning I heard—
Every morning
Every evening
Don't we have fun!

In 1920 as today, infant arrivals provided the best hope for fresh beginnings, even at times of financial turmoil. Those hopes don't fade because someone else's kid achieved epochal success in some other corner of the economy. Every family's new generation stands a chance of producing an earth-altering entrepreneur, until they show us differently. As Brooks writes, "The fact that Bill Gates is so rich probably raises the happiness of America's optimists, because it demonstrates to them what somebody can do with hard work, good ideas, great luck, and a system that protects free enterprise. Gates is not a duke or a prince; there is no evidence that God especially likes him. He simply had a lot of opportunities and made the most of them."

All attempts to foster resentment of success ultimately will fail in the United States. As the sardonic (and left-leaning) essayist Fran Lebowitz observes, "Oh, please, Americans do not hate the rich; they want to be them. Every American believes that they are the impending rich, and that will never change."

"Business Executives
Are Overpaid and Corrupt"

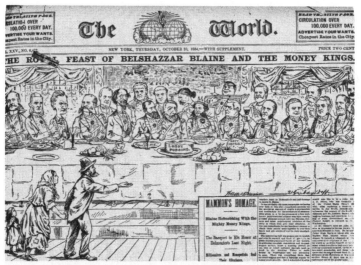

Belshazzar Blaine and the Money Kings at Delmonico's. (*New York World*, Oct. 30, 1884.)

"CRIMES AGAINST HUMILITY"

In June 2001, a giant ice sculpture that urinated premium vodka became a lurid symbol of twenty-first-century executive excess.

This huge frozen effigy, incongruously modeled on the classical Michelangelo sculpture of the biblical David, served as the dominant decoration in a laughably lavish birthday bash for the new wife of Dennis Kozlowski, hard-charging CEO of the gigantic health care and electronics conglomerate Tyco. Kozlowski had first met his adored soulmate, Karen Mayo, while she worked as a waitress in Ron's Beach House, a high-end watering hole near corporate headquarters in Exeter, New Hampshire. They began keeping company while inconveniently married to others, but managed to shed spouses (and inhibitions) before their romantic nuptials on Antigua in May 2001. A month later, the Tyco Titan planned a much splashier celebration at an exclusive private club on the Italian island of Sardinia to mark the fortieth birthday of his blond, flashy, freshly minted life partner.

The party details included scores of leggy fashion models dressed as Roman "slave girls" in skimpy tunics, along with loincloth-clad body-builders portraying gladiators. A company employee spelled out the arrangements in advance in a memo that later became infamous:

> Guests arrive at the club starting at 7.15 p.m. The van pulls up to the main entrance. Two gladiators are standing next to the door, one opens the door, the other helps the guests. We have a lion or horse with a chariot for the shock value. The guests proceed through the two rooms. We have gladiators standing guard every couple feet and they are lining the way. The guests come into the pool area, the band is playing, they are dressed in elegant chic. Big ice sculpture of David, lots of shellfish and caviar at his feet. A waiter is pouring Stoli vodka into his back so it comes out his penis into a crystal glass.

Meanwhile, "waiters are passing cocktails in chalices. They are dressed in linen togas with fig wreath on head. A full bar with fabulous linens. The pool has floating candles and flowers. We have rented fig trees with tiny lights everywhere to fill some space." The climax came with "Elvis" on a big screen wishing Karen happy birthday before "a huge cake is brought out with the waiters in togas singing and holding the cake up for all to see. The tits explode, Elvis kicks it in full throttle."

The last two details sound downright alarming, but not so frightening, perhaps, as the tab for the bacchanal: some $2 million in various fees for the evening's entertainment, with a cool million paid in corporate funds. Because numerous shareholders attended the peerlessly tacky proceedings, Kozlowski and associates chose to classify it as a company event. In a camcorder video captured on site, the fig-wreathed host proudly declared that the party would "bring out" a "Tyco core competency—the ability to party hard!"

The specifics of the birthday blowout eventually became a media obsession, together with costly tchotchkes chosen by a decorator and billed to the company in order to spruce up a corporate Manhattan apartment the Kozlowskis almost never used. The press inevitably focused on a $6,000 shower curtain in the maid's bathroom, a $15,000 umbrella stand, and a $17,000 traveling toilette box whose contributions to the firm's productivity or profitability remained difficult to explain.

The fun and funding both came to an end on June 17, 2005 (almost exactly four years after the shindig in Sardinia), with the conviction of Dennis Kozlowski for misappropriation of Tyco's funds. In his second trial, prosecutors won convictions on twenty-two counts of grand larceny for $150 million in unauthorized bonuses and additional fraud against corporate shareholders. The onetime captain of industry now captains a dreary six-foot-by-ten-foot cell in the Mid-State Correctional

Facility in Marcy, New York, where he's serving a minimum sentence of eight years, four months. To the amazement of virtually no one, his wife Karen sued for divorce less than a year after his sentence began; the marriage that had been celebrated with a Roman orgy "for the ages" actually endured barely five years. When asked in a jailhouse interview why his glamorous wife had left him, a chastened Kozlowski simply stated, "[B]ecause I'm no longer a rich, powerful CEO. . . . If I was a poor production laborer, or struggling as a reporter for a newspaper, I don't think Karen would have had any interest in me whatsoever. I was an easy guy for a woman to fall in love with at that time when I was at the top of my game. But I did not want to admit that. My first wife told me that was what was going on and she was right."

During Kozlowski's headline-making trials, the press treated his melodramatic rise and fall as emblematic of the intemperate, corrupt corporate culture of an entire era. The simultaneous and spectacular collapse of fraudulent, high-flying companies like Enron and WorldCom made it easy to associate Kozlowski with those horrendously damaging scandals, even though Tyco easily survived his alleged "looting" of the company. Ken Lay and Bernie Ebbers, the celebrated CEOs who received their own long prison terms for masterminding the Enron and WorldCom scams, devastated literally tens of thousands of employees and shareholders, while fellow jailbird Kozlowski committed mostly "crimes against humility" (as wags commented at the time) and dealt only glancing blows to the company he served. Regardless of the complex legal issues in his two trials, Kozlowski's beleaguered friends and apologists insisted that their guy didn't deserve classification with the most notorious firm-wreckers and outright frauds of corporate America. Within a year of his resignation in 2002, Tyco had returned to robust growth and profitability and today continues to provide jobs for 120,000 employees around the world. The product of a working-class, Polish-American home in the gritty Central Ward of Newark, New Jersey, Kozlowski scrapped his way to the top by toiling for Tyco for twenty-seven years; his decade as chairman and CEO saw the aggressive acquisition of numerous enterprises, prodigious growth in revenue, and the reliable outperformance of Wall Street expectations.

His personal peccadilloes clearly displayed poor judgment and weak character, but they hardly count as emblematic of a whole business system gone wrong or help to explain the recent economic crisis. Kozlowski and his most notorious corporate colleagues drew intensive press attention because they were exceptional, not typical. Evidence and experience show that the real life demands of American business encourage self-discipline over indulgence and reliability over arrogance.

LUDICROUSLY OVERPAID PARASITES

Nevertheless, publicity for executive extravagance (even without flamboyant touches like vodka-spewing ice sculptures) always serves to reinforce the notion that corporate chieftains constitute a class of selfish, shallow, preposterously pampered, and ludicrously overpaid parasites.

The public fury over multimillion-dollar executive compensation packages recently reached such feverish and bilious intensity that even conservative politicians began suggesting that some of those greedy business leaders actually deserve to die. In March 2009, Senator Charles Grassley of Iowa (ranking Republican on the Finance Committee) noted that the American International Group (AIG) had received some $180 billion in a series of government bailouts, but still found $165 million to pay out in bonuses to some of its top officials. In an interview with an Iowa radio station, the senator suggested that the conspicuously well-compensated AIG brass should "follow the Japanese example and come before the American people and take that deep bow and say, I'm sorry, and then do one of two things: resign or go commit suicide."

With no real enthusiasm for either retirement or hara-kiri, the leaders of AIG declined the chance to follow his advice while tactfully describing the Grassley remarks as "very disappointing." Those remarks, after all, looked moderate and constructive when compared with the flat-out advocacy of the death penalty for corporate greed from English professor Kurt Hochenauer of the University of Central Oklahoma in his rousing call to arms, "Let Wall Street Die": "Let their deaths be merciless. No taxpayer bailout . . . should go to rescue the growing cesspool of filthy-rich, elite financial managers whose unchecked greed and false sense of entitlement has given this country its worst financial crisis since the Great Depression."

Meanwhile, the raging hysteria over Wall Street bonuses in the midst of economic crisis strengthened the public's suspicion that the most influential and admired leaders of the business community had abandoned all sense of decency and decorum. Shortly after the initial round of government bailouts, the annual Gallup poll "Honesty and Ethics of Professions" (November 2008) showed only 1 percent who rated the "honesty and ethical standards" of "business executives" as "very high," while 37 percent graded them as "very low" or "low." Such frequently suspect categories as "lawyers," "journalists," and "bankers" scored notably better than "business executives"—not to mention widely admired professions such as "nurses," "clergy," "medical doctors," and "policemen." Even before the financial meltdown, with the economy growing and the federal deficit declining, overwhelming majorities of Americans believed that top corporate honchos received far more compensation than they deserved. Some 80 percent of respondents polled by Bloomberg and the *Los Angeles Times* in 2006 agreed that "CEO's are overpaid." This proposition commanded huge majorities of every component of the population, regardless of income or political affiliation.

During periods of economic hardship, corporate leaders inevitably inspire rage and resentment, because they seem so powerfully isolated from the suffering that afflicts the rest of us; during years of growth and prosperity they draw comparable hostility for their "disproportionate" or showy share of national success. When the economy goes down, it's easy—and almost irresistible—to blame business leaders. When indicators turn upward, on the other hand, those executives rarely get credit. Conventional wisdom associates economic recovery and boom times with natural cycles or the plans and programs of some popular politician. We assume that progress occurs in spite of the greed and selfishness of corporate bosses, with no real connection to their pursuit of profit.

For instance, in February 1996, at the very core of what we now remember as the "Clinton Boom," *Newsweek* ran an ominous cover story entitled "Corporate Killers." The featured images showed prominent business bosses like Robert Allen of AT&T and Louis Gerstner of IBM in altered photographs designed to resemble criminal mug shots. The accusation against these "hit men" involved massive layoffs: "Call it 'in your face capitalism.' You lose your job, your ex-employer's stock price rises, and the CEO gets a fat raise. Something is just plain wrong when stock prices keep rising on Wall Street while Main Street is littered with the bodies of workers discarded by the big companies."

Aside from fudging the obvious if inconvenient fact that laid-off employees don't generally "litter" their hometowns by dying on the sidewalk, the *Newsweek* piece (by Allan Sloan) utterly ignores the context of the job losses it describes. As my friend Daniel Lapin points out in his insightful bestseller *Thou Shall Prosper,* the cover story about corporate mass murder came at the conclusion of one of the most notable periods of job growth in American economic history. "Between 1991 and 1995, the number of Americans newly employed had grown by 7.2 million," Lapin writes. "In other words, while some companies were shedding workers, other companies were hiring workers; and far more people were being newly hired than fired. *Newsweek* stated that a total of 137,000 workers had lost their jobs in the companies highlighted in the story and held the story's Corporate Killers responsible for the loss. Yet *Newsweek* failed to mention that the U.S. economy during that period was adding 137,000 jobs *every three weeks!*"

The idea that guilty businessmen (and, every once in a while, guilty businesswomen) cause all the world's problems has become so widely accepted that it's infected even many of those who choose to make their lives in corporate America. Marianne Jennings, a professor of legal and ethical studies at the College of Business at Arizona State University, noted in the *Wall Street Journal* (May 3, 1999) that "many of my students are deeply offended by high levels of executive pay, deplore stock options, and believe that a company's gay-rights position is a litmus test

CORPORATE CHARITY:
INSPIRING, OR INAPPROPRIATE?

In the midst of a severe economic downturn, business leaders have mobilized for an intensified emphasis on corporate philanthropy. According to *The Chronicle of Philanthropy* (February 24, 2009), in some struggling companies executives decided to experiment by authorizing their employees to commit to a weekly "afternoon of service" while trying to "step up volunteerism and explore other non-cash ways of helping charities." A recent survey also showed a marked increase in corporate giving to international causes, despite the economic hard times.

Meanwhile, Yaron Brook of the Ayn Rand Institute offered a powerful challenge to the whole idea of corporations "giving back" through charitable endeavors. "Profit-making is virtue, not vice," he wrote for Businessweek.com (June 2008). "Productive businesses deserve the money they earn. Their wealth is created, not taken from those who didn't produce it, so there exists nothing to 'give back.' . . . And yet, our culture views profit as distasteful and offensive, a cause for apology and repentance. Productive businesspeople have been told they must wash off the moral stain of profit-seeking through community service, as by manning soup kitchens in the slums or digging latrines in Africa. . . . Yes, there's a moral debt involved, but it runs the opposite way. It's each individual's obligation to recognize that profit-seeking is a virtue, and to acknowledge it publicly as such. Such moral support costs nothing, but its value for promoting justice is inestimable."

for morality. . . . They believe that business spawned the homeless. They take it for granted that businesses cheat and are oddly
resigned to it."

"344-TO-1"

According to embittered critics of the market system, the most
glaring evidence of that cheating and corruption comes from
the swelling pay disparity between workers and bosses. In a stri-
dent 2007 "Green Festival" speech cheerfully titled "The Road to
Corporate Fascism," four-time presidential candidate Ralph
Nader declared, "The Corporate System is inherently defective,
no matter how it grows, no matter where it grows. It will not
just damage the environment and cheat consumers, and provide hazardous work places, et cetera, but it will cycle the gains
back into the top 5, 4, 3, 2, 1 percent. When I was growing up in
a factory town in Connecticut, the heads of these factories, not
one of them was making more than seven times the worker
wage in their factory. And I'm talking about the top guys, not
the managers. Now, it's the Fortune 500 CEO's are making 400
to 500 times more than the average worker. The head of Walmart made $11,000 an hour and hundreds of thousands of his
workers were making 6, 7, 8 dollars an hour. You can see the gap
growing, growing. There isn't even a word to describe it. Calling
it a 'gap' is not enough."

Of course there's no evidence at all that cutting the compensation of Walmart CEO Mike Duke would magically raise the
wages of his 2,100,000 employees, but levelers like Ralph Nader
pay far more attention to the privileges of those at the top of the
corporate ladder than they do to the welfare and advancement

of those at the bottom. According to the Census Bureau, median household income went up from $41,613 in 1982 (in inflation-adjusted dollars) to $49,233 in 2007—a hefty increase of more than 20 percent and providing a significant addition of $8,620. At the same time, the earnings of the typical CEO as compared with those of an average U.S. worker went up from 30-to-1 (never the nostalgically remembered 7-to-1 recalled by Ralph Nader) all the way to 344-to-1, according to the liberal advocacy group United for a Fair Economy in a much-discussed 2007 study.

The *L.A. Times* reported that the ratio of CEO compensation to the average worker's salary had risen even higher—to an all-time peak of 525-to-1—in 2000, thanks to lucrative options and a soaring stock market. Most recently, the trend has brought executive pay packages closer to the salaries of typical workers, not increased the disparity. This shrinking of the infamous pay gap actually corresponds with *Forbes* magazine figures in April 2009 showing a sharp drop in chief executive compensation at the 500 biggest U.S. companies—down 15 percent in 2007, and another 11 percent in 2008, for the first two-year back-to-back pay hit since 2001 and 2002, even at a time when remuneration for average workers went up. (The Department of Labor reported that the national average weekly income rose 2.5 percent, from $598 in 2007 to $613 in 2008.) This doesn't mean that suffering CEOs deserve the pity of the public, or that the slight improvements for working-class employees somehow pinched their proceeds, or that schoolchildren need to take up collections of dimes and quarters to reduce their misery; with average pay packages of $11.4 million in 2008 (according to *Forbes*), these big bosses could endure even more substantive reductions in the years ahead without serious threat to their luxurious living standards.

Nevertheless, the unheralded but significant decline in executive compensation (in both absolute terms and as a multiple of the salaries of average employees) exposes one of the most irresponsible fictions about contemporary American business. It also gives the lie to the widespread, destructive notion that typical corporate heads bring home ever more outrageous pay packages even while the public at large (not to mention stockholders and employees) suffers the ravages of severe recession. While a few highly publicized leaders of troubled firms—Stanley O'Neal of Merrill Lynch, Charles O. Prince of Citigroup, John J. Mack of Morgan Stanley—have walked away with gigantic rewards or settlements despite the wretched performance of their companies, researchers have begun to discern a more reasonable trend in executive compensation. *Financial Week* reported a major study by Equilar (the executive compensation research firm) showing that the median value of performance-based bonuses for CEOs in large public firms went down in 2007 (even before the economic meltdown) from $949,249 to $772,717, a dramatic decrease of 18.6 percent

More recently, Madhukar Angur, professor of marketing at the Flint campus of the University of Michigan, examined executive compensation at top U.S. corporations and found little evidence of systemic plunder of big companies by greedy CEOs. As he wrote in *Investor's Business Daily* (March 23, 2009), "Recent research, however, suggests that this abuse of corporate finances may not be as prevalent as it seems. Indeed, over 40 percent of the 94 U.S. corporations I have studied had CEO compensation generally based on proportionate increase or decrease in the

LIVES OF TOIL AND STRESS, NOT SELF-INDULGENCE

In pop culture, images of wealthy executives usually connect them with yachts and swimming pools, golf courses and ski lodges, Gulfstreams, and absurdly expensive restaurants. A more accurate portrayal would stress long hours, punishing stress, BlackBerry interruptions, lost sleep, and missed family occasions. In groundbreaking work that he described in the *New York Times,* Dalton Conley, chair of the sociology department at New York University, reveals that "it is now the rich who are the most stressed out and the most likely to be working the most. Perhaps for the first time since we've kept track of such things, higher-income folks work more hours than lower-wage earners do." In his *Times* column (September 2, 2008), Conley also referenced a study by economists Peter Kuhn and Fernando Lozano, showing that since 1980 the number of men in the bottom fifth of the income scale who work long hours (defined as more than 49 hours per week) dropped by half. At the same time, long weeks for the top fifth of earners increased a painful 80 percent.

"Today, the more we earn the more we work, since the opportunity cost of not working is all the greater," Conley concludes. "In other words, when we get a raise, instead of using that hard-won money to buy 'the good life,' we feel even more pressure to work since the shadow costs of not working are all the greater." A supporting study by Daniel Hamermesh and Jungmin Lee shows that women with higher incomes (purportedly leading pampered lives and relying on hired help) actually report feeling more stressed than women with lower incomes. More money doesn't necessarily produce more comfort and leisure, but increases the sense of responsibility and challenge—the desire to use every available moment in a productive and beneficial way.

Daniel Gross, insightful and fearless columnist for *Newsweek* and Slate (and a repeat guest on my radio show), reached similar conclusions in a fascinating piece, "No Rest for the Wealthy," in the *New York Times Book Review* (July 5, 2009). "In the contemporary money culture, to be at leisure, to be idle, is to be irrelevant. . . . A great many people can afford not to work and could spend their time shuttling between multiple homes, eating fabulous meals and playing golf. Yet they continue to work around the clock. . . . Among Type-A, self-made members of the leisure class, there's a sort of reverse prestige associated with leisure." Gross noted that the yearly World Economic Forum at the glorious Alpine resort of Davos allowed few of the movers and shakers to relax. "At Davos, which is filled with conspicuous consumers, the only people who ski are the journalists."

In other words, an all-consuming ethic of effort and a constitutional allergy to wasted time contribute significantly to the well-publicized success of most leaders of American business. These CEOs, as well as most middle managers, affirm the eternal connection between economic advancement and hard work.

company's net worth or paid less to CEOs despite an increase in company net worth." Professor Angur saw this surprising tendency to cut CEO pay even when they led thriving companies as a healthy sign of an economic system swinging back to balance and shareholder control. "Given that nearly a third of the top Fortune 100 companies paid less compensation to their CEOs despite an increase in the companies' net worth, that suggests that the threatening economy has kick-started corporate governance and other self-regulatory systems in a significant number of U.S. companies. If this trend continues, the nation will see more companies tying CEO compensation to corporate performance. The end results might be more sustainable business and renewed public trust."

"YOU DO GET WHAT YOU PAY FOR"

Critics of corporate power and CEO privilege will naturally scoff at such minor adjustments. To them, it hardly matters if the ratio of executive compensation to worker salary declines from 525-to-1 to 344-to-1 in the most recent decade: annual pay packages that top $10 million for corporate brass still look irrational, indulgent, and obscene, especially in the midst of economic hard times. The question isn't whether the payment to big bosses will continue to soar or gradually settle back down to earth. For the general public, the biggest mystery involves how corporate board members and concerned stockholders could have ever let the compensation packages rise so high in the first place.

One savvy and respected observer from the left side of the political spectrum takes the courageous position that the breathtaking increase in CEO compensation actually makes perfect sense, given deeper changes in the American marketplace. "There's an economic case for the stratospheric level of

CEO pay which suggests shareholders—even if they had full say—would not reduce it," writes Robert Reich, the outspoken labor secretary under Bill Clinton and now a professor of public policy at the University of California at Berkeley. In the *Wall Street Journal* (September 14, 2007) he predicted that these shareholders were "likely to let CEO pay continue to soar. That's because of a fundamental shift in the structure of the economy over the last four decades, from oligopolistic capitalistic to super-competitive capitalism. CEO pay has risen astronomically over the interval, but so have investor returns."

Reich perceptively compares the corporate heads of today with those who ran major companies in the 1950s and '60s, when even the most powerful business leader "was mostly a bureaucrat in charge of a large, high-volume production system whose rules were standardized and whose competitors were docile. It was the era of stable oligopolies, big unions, predictable markets and lackluster share performance. The CEO of a modern company is in a different situation. Oligopolies are mostly gone and entry barriers are low. Rivals are impinging all the time—threatening to lure away consumers all too willing to be lured away, and threatening to hijack investors eager to jump ship at the slightest hint of an upturn in a rival's share price."

He compares the shift to the much-discussed changes in the movie business. Fifty years ago, eight big studios utterly dominated the United States market, shutting out all would-be competitors and comfortably dividing the available audience among them. These secure, well-established companies became household names, signing the biggest stars to long-term, exclusive contracts and thereby limiting their competition. As Reich notes, "Clark Gable earned $100,000 a picture in the 1940s, roughly $800,000 in present dollars. But that was when Hollywood was dominated by big-studio oligopolies. Today, Tom Hanks makes closer to $20 million per film. Movie studios—now competing intensely not only with one another but with every other form of entertainment—willingly pay these sums because they're still small compared to the money these stars bring in and profits they generate. Today's big companies are paying their CEOs mammoth sums for much the same reason."

Secretary Reich cites the storied (and controversial) payout to Lee R. Raymond, chairman of ExxonMobil, who retired in 2005 with a compensation package totaling nearly $400 million, including stock, stock options, and long-term compensation. "Too much?" Reich asks. "Not to Exxon's investors, who enjoyed a 223 percent return over the interval, compared to the average 205 percent return received by shareholders of other oil companies, a premium of about $16 billion. Raymond took home just 4 percent of that $16 billion."

In other words, under the circumstances, even a payday of nearly half a billion dollars can represent a real bargain for exceptionally gifted (or lucky) CEOs. Madhukar Angur notes that "using company net worth as the basis of performance measures, Jack Welch, the former CEO of General Electric, is considered underpaid." Welch, named "Manager of the Century" by *Fortune* magazine in 1999, earned a salary of "only" $4 million in 2001, his final year at GE. Meanwhile, Professor Angur observes, "his unique leadership style and business acumen . . . took the company's worth from about $14 billion in 1981 to $500 billion just before retiring."

As Robert Murphy noted at Townhall.com (September 15, 2007), "In our increasingly global economy, certain individuals are incredibly productive and can command incredibly high earnings as a result. Corporate executives really do perform valuable tasks, and it really does make a difference who is running the company. Once we concede that productive individuals will earn more than less productive ones, the fact that some make 364 times what others do is largely irrelevant. After all, a TV set might be 364 times more expensive than a gumball. Is that 'unfair' or does it merely reflect the forces of supply and demand?"

The operation of those forces inevitably impels executive compensation to levels that disturb the public. In *Forbes* magazine (February 19, 2009), Marc Hodak, who teaches corporate governance at New York University's Leonard N. Stern School of Business, described his own experience negotiating major contracts for corporate leaders. "I would be perfectly happy living in a world where the typical CEO made no more than, say, 30 times the pay of the average worker," he confessed. "I don't think anyone needs more than that to be happy or secure, or deserves more than that as an expression of their value to humanity. I'm also a compensation consultant that shareholders hire to get the best executives at the lowest prices. I don't pay more than I have to, but I often have to pay more than 30 times what the average worker makes. You do get what you pay for."

Hodak sympathizes with the sense of outrage that afflicts lower-level employees at major companies with head honchos who earn millions. "I know it's hard for someone making $50,000 a year to imagine that anyone can be worth 10 or a hundred times that. But they might be. How do I know? Because if I don't pay them, someone else will. When an executive across the table tells me, 'The guys down the street are offering $2 million a year,' he's not bluffing. The experienced buyer of managerial talent can see the difference between a $500,000 executive and a $2 million executive as surely as a home buyer can tell the difference between a half-million-dollar home and a $2 million home."

My former law school classmate Robert Reich—who has argued for forty years for activist government, higher tax rates, and closer corporate regulation—nonetheless recognizes that executive salaries reflect basic realities of supply and demand rather than the back-scratching indulgence of some insider old-boy network. "The pool of proven talent is small because so few executives have been tested and succeeded," he writes in the *Wall Street Journal.* "And the boards of major companies do not want to risk error. The cost of recruiting the wrong person can be very large—and readily apparent in the deteriorating value of a company's share. Boards are willing to pay more and more for CEO's and other top executives because their rivals are paying more and more for them."

As both a Berkeley academic and a former member of the Clinton cabinet, Reich has never been shy about deploying the power of federal bureaucracy to achieve some worthy goal, but he shuns the idea of utilizing such a mechanism to limit compensation packages in the business world. Not even the most ambitious and audacious reformer would support the notion of forcing salaries and bonuses to match some concept of the intrinsic worth of work. As Rob Preston argues in *InformationWeek* (January 13, 2007), "If salaries were just about the importance or perils of the work, teachers and nurses and power plant technicians and soldiers would be pulling down the big bucks. That they're not doesn't mean they're any less critical; it just means that employers could find more of them at the pay they now earn. Water is cheap because it's abundant. Gold is expensive because it's not. Which is the more critical commodity?"

"MOST VALUABLE BOSSES"

At a time of economic pain and insecurity, populist outrage inevitably focuses on corporate leaders who pocket huge paychecks despite the wretched performance of their companies. For instance, since Kenneth D. Lewis took over as top executive of Bank of America in April 2001, the firm's annual return of −8 percent (as reported by *Forbes* magazine) significantly trailed the record of the S&P 500, but Lewis has received compensation that averages more than $30 million annually.

Fortunately, many other bosses offer a wholesome contrast to the well-publicized instances of lavish pay for poor performance. Since 2002, *Forbes* has compiled an annual scorecard of performance versus pay to select those executives whose achievements represent the most conspicuous bargains for investors. At the top of this "Most Valuable Bosses" list for 2009 was Michael L. Bennett of Terra Industries, a chemical company specializing in nitrogen compounds. Over the last six years, he delivered an eye-popping annual return to shareholders of 64 percent. His payment during that period of spectacular growth averaged a relatively modest $3.5 million (including salary and other benefits).

Another example of an apparently underpaid executive is Jeff Bezos of Amazon.com, who has generated an annualized total return during his career with the company of 40 percent. During the last six years, however, he took total annual compensation of "only" a million dollars a year. Since he also owns 24 percent of Amazon stock, it's probably inappropriate to feel pity for Bezos, who still places 110th on the *Forbes* list of world billionaires.

Two weeks later, Preston continued his defense of the fundamental rationality of the employment market, when allowed to operate with minimal interference, and insisted that CEO compensation packages "are more often a function of the incontrovertible forces of supply and demand than of nepotism, negligence, incompetence, deception, fraud, or some other scheme. . . . The fact remains that most of that compensation is dispensed in an open competitive market. If shareholders don't like what the CEO or other top execs are pulling down, they can vote with their feet or apply direct pressure on the board of directors, as a Home Depot investor group did, leading to the recent ouster of CEO Robert Nardelli."

Of course, Nardelli managed to leave the firm with an "exit package" totaling $210 million, but Preston insists "that was part of the price of luring him from GE, where he was a star under Jack Welch. A contract is a contract. Could Home Depot have found cheaper talent? Sure, but Nardelli was considered one of the nation's top execs at the time. And while his arrogance may have done him in at Home Depot, he was no slouch, doubling the company's sales and more than doubling its earnings per share during his six-year tenure, while creating 100,000 net new jobs."

THE VALUE OF STEVE JOBS'S LIVER

No business story of recent years more dramatically illustrated the importance of that one guy at the top than the worldwide reaction to the critical illness of Apple cofounder Steve Jobs. On January 15, 2009, the announcement that the survivor of pancreatic cancer planned to take a six-month medical leave of absence made the front page of *USA Today* and many other newspapers across the country. The story by Jon Swartz and Byron Acohido reported that "jittery investors reacted immediately to Jobs' medical leave, sending Apple shares down 7 percent, to $79.30, in after-hours trading—its lowest in two years. . . . His medical leave, however long, raises questions about Apple's long-term viability. . . . 'You don't replace Steve Jobs,' says Brian Sullivan, CEO of executive search firm CTPartners. 'You slice up what he does: product development, vision and marketing. No one person can bring his swagger and savoir-faire to Apple.'"

Would it make sense for the company to spare any expense to keep their corporate star healthy and on the scene? Would anyone suggest that Apple overpaid Steve Jobs, considering his direct, undeniable impact on its share price and prospects? His leadership seemed so essential to the firm's continued success and the welfare of its 35,000 employees that Warren Buffett (and many others) criticized Jobs's colleagues for not disclosing more information about his medical condition. On CNBC, the Sage of Omaha commented, "If I have any serious illness, or something coming up of an important nature, an operation or anything like that, I think the thing to do is just tell the American people, the Berkshire shareholders about it. I work for 'em. Some people might think I'm important to the company. Certainly Steve Jobs is important to Apple. So it's a material fact."

When Jobs returned from his leave in June, disclosing that he had undergone a successful liver transplant in Tennessee, the *New York Times* noted that concerns over the health of the boss meant that "Apple shares fell despite the company announcing that it had sold more than a million units of its latest iPhone model in the first three days." The British newspaper *The Independent* described the "nosedive" of Apple stock and related the

decline of the business leader's uncanny and seemingly super-
natural power. "Those who know him well say he has radiated a
'mesmeric presence' his entire adult life; that he is a charismatic
visionary who is solely responsible for creating personal computers," wrote Caitriona Palmer. "He is 'the most powerful person I've ever met. The word charisma—in the true, Greek sense
of grace or gift—applies. He has the power to open up your
chest and put his fingers inside you,' said Jean-Louis Gassée,
chief of product development at Apple."

The relentless focus on Jobs's influence, imagination, magical
command abilities, and significance for an entire industry drew
sardonic comment from columnist David Carr in the *New York
Times* (July 6, 2009): "Next February, when Steven P. Jobs—
knock on wood—does his big reveal at Macworld, the geegaw
people will most want to see probably won't be on display. He
will not reveal his pancreas so that the horde can examine it for
signs of recurring cancer. There won't be a JumboTron image of
his recently transplanted liver so that they might turn it over
with a stick as they look for signs of rejection. And despite the
fever for all things Mac, there won't be an iPhone app that tracks
Mr. Jobs's health in real time, including blood sugar, blood pressure and white blood cell count."

While Steve Jobs proved chronically reluctant to discuss his
personal prognosis or his significance to the company he
founded, another high-tech titan clearly understood what he
meant to his own gargantuan enterprise.

A few years ago, one of our close friends in Seattle worked
for Microsoft and encountered the company's cofounder and
current chairman, Bill Gates, during one of his periodic tours
of the Redmond, Washington, campus. As the boss and his en-
tourage bustled into her building early one morning, greeting a

few of the startled employees, he walked directly toward our friend in the human resources division—perhaps because she's pretty, petite, and an obvious live wire. As he approached, the world's wealthiest human posed a challenging question: "So, what have you accomplished for our company so far this morning?"

Without apology or pause, our friend replied, "I'm not sure, Mr. Gates, but what have you accomplished today?"

This cheeky response brought nervous laughter from the Gates aides and associates who overheard it, but the great man himself barely cracked a smile, pausing for just a moment before delivering his serious answer. "You want to know what I accomplished? I got up today. That's what I did. I got out of bed. And I even came into work. And don't think that isn't important to you and everybody else."

He's right, of course. Even though Gates no longer takes direct responsibility for day-to-day operations at Microsoft (he handed responsibility to Ray Ozzie and Craig Mundie in 2006 so he could concentrate on the international operations of his charitable foundation), the company and its 90,000 worldwide employees still depend on his public association, occasional presence, and overall guidance. Were he to disappear suddenly from the scene through illness, or lack of interest, or some unexpected desire to enter a monastery in Tibet, the separation from a brand he created would shake investor confidence and impact the company's future. Though Gates (like important executives in other leading corporations) takes limited salary and draws most of his compensation through stock, no one could question the proposition that he meant more to the operation's success than the combined efforts of 344 lower-level employees— or 3,440 of them, for that matter.

HOW MUCH PER HOMER?

Since most Americans (or at least most male Americans) understand sports better than they understand business, it makes sense to relate the multimillion-dollar compensation for corporate stars to the multimillion-dollar contracts and signing bonuses for stars of basketball, football, and baseball. Lavish spending for expensive free agents is always a gamble, but even if it doesn't pay off in terms of winning more games (the equivalent of a company enhancing revenue or profitability), it will probably deliver value in terms of stimulating fan interest and ticket sales (comparable to improved investor confidence and rising stock prices).

The most generously paid player in baseball, Alex Rodriguez, will receive $33 million to play third base for the New York Yankees in 2009 (nearly a third more than Manny Ramirez of the Dodgers, who's second on the list), but he failed to lead his team to the playoffs last year and has earned a reputation for failing to deliver "clutch" hits in big games. A-Rod, despite scandals involving unhealthful indulgence in dangerous substances such as steroids and Madonna, receives twice as much as Albert Pujols of the St. Louis Cardinals, whose career batting average of .334 easily eclipses the Rodriguez figure of .305. What's more, Pujols leads the major leagues in virtue—as an exemplary family man, outspoken Christian, and prodigiously generous benefactor of charities for Down syndrome kids.

By what logic, then, does A-Rod deserve vastly higher levels or remuneration than the incomparable first baseman for the Red Birds? In part, he earns more dough because he plays in a much bigger market for a much richer team, and attendance figures show he helps lure more fans to the new Yankee Stadium (in part, no doubt, to boo the slugger). It's certainly arguable that the Yankees overpaid by a few million, but it's not possible that A-Rod would fail to bring home some huge contract from one of the richer teams. The New Yorkers re-signed him in part to prevent his desertion to their eternal enemies, the Boston Red Sox.

The millions of Americans who play fantasy baseball understand that the most accomplished and charismatic stars are worth any number of rookies or journeymen. On occasion, teams (in both fantasy leagues and reality) agree to terms that make no sense at all in retrospect. In 2007, my own beloved Seattle Mariners shelled out $15.5 million to a 6′8″, strikeout-prone giant named Richie Sexson, making him twelfth on the list of the top-paid players in baseball. He responded by hitting an appalling .205 and clubbing only twenty-one home runs—which led to calculations that the Ms (who finished in last place that year) paid 740,000 bucks per dinger. This represented a notably poor investment, but "Sexsie" has since disappeared from major-league baseball, as well as the team payroll.

The market, in other words, provides its own rough justice, though even the smartest baseball heads in the world will occasionally agree to ill-considered contracts. By the same token, major businesses will get involved in bidding wars to lure key executives with irresponsibly generous deals, only to see some highly touted CEO slugger whiffing repeatedly in crucial situations while contributing to a losing season. Nevertheless, in baseball as in business, big-name achievers generally continue to achieve. This means more in the corporate world, of course: in competitive sports, the number of teams who make it to the playoffs or league championship series remains strictly limited, but in business any number of companies can simultaneously succeed, all enjoying championship seasons in a period of generalized growth.

UNDERSTANDING BONUS BABIES

The sports analogy also helps to explain the perplexing question of executive bonuses, even in times of corporate turmoil or with major losses on the ledger books. In baseball, bonuses often connect to individualized achievement—a Cy Young Award, or selection for the All-Star Team, or forty home runs. On occasion, these accomplishments occur even on losing teams: in 2009, third baseman Ryan Zimmerman made his first trip to the All-Star Game and compiled impressive statistics, despite playing for the Washington Nationals, who had by far the worst record in baseball. No one would suggest that Zimmerman forgo performance bonuses because his team is thirty games out of first place, or losing money for its investors.

Similarly, it makes sense and follows the dictates of basic fairness to pay out promised performance bonuses at troubled financial companies, even if the firms themselves show no profit. Without such incentives for individual executives, struggling businesses might lose even more money and face a tougher time in making a comeback. Roy C. Smith, professor of finance at New York University, defended the rewards policy in the *Wall Street Journal* (February 7, 2008): "Lost in the denunciations were the powerful benefits of the bonus system, which helped make the U.S. the global leader in financial services for decades. Bonuses are an important and necessary part of the fast-moving, high-pressure industry and its employees flourish with strong performance incentives."

Compensation consultant Marc Hodak helped put the bonus controversy into proper perspective (*Forbes,* February 19, 2009): "Most of what we call 'bonuses' on Wall Street actually resembles commission earned by a modestly salaried salesperson, albeit with a very high upside. No one familiar with how salespeople get paid would consider zero commissions in a bad year as a sensible outcome. Even if the salesperson sold only half what he sold last year, he still deserves some commission. That's where the 'shameful' $18 billion in bonuses went—to traders whose books did not blow up, investment banks who squeezed some fees from a desiccated market, and asset managers whose portfolios survived the carnage relatively intact. . . . A billion dollars is a lot of money to anyone who isn't a U.S. congressman. But because the vast majority of Citigroup's workers, those who had nothing to do with toxic mortgages or auction-rate securities, still had the prospect of at least some bonuses, they still had an incentive to keep overall company losses from getting worse. Absent those bonuses that caused Wall Street so much grief, Citigroup could have easily lost many billions more with the shareholders never knowing how preventable those losses might have been."

For all the political and media outrage at bonus payments (including Senator Grassley's suggestion of suicide), legislative efforts to cap or redirect executive compensation almost always backfire. On September 26, 2008, the *Los Angeles Times* ran the revealing headline "Attempts to Limit CEO Pay Have Yet to Succeed." The solid reporting by Jim Puzzanghera went back to Bill Clinton's efforts to make executive salaries a major issue in the campaign of 1992. He contacted Graef Crystal, a former compensation consultant and author of six books on the subject, and laid out a proposal to limit a corporation's authorization to deduct for tax purposes anything over $1 million in salary. Crystal immediately warned Clinton it wouldn't work, but the candidate pressed forward with the idea after his election. As the *Times* story explains, "The resulting law, which was passed in 1993, is widely believed to have led to the explosion in stock options for executives as companies sought ways to avoid the salary restriction. Total CEO compensation surged through the rest of the decade, to 300 times the average worker's salary in 2000 from 100 times the average in 1993, according to the Economic Policy Institute, a liberal think tank."

Many financial insiders predict similar unintended consequences from any effort to restrict bonuses. Marc Hodak writes, "If we're bent on ridding Wall Street of those dreaded bonuses, banks will have to replace bonus opportunities with much higher fixed salaries than they now pay in order to remain competitive. In a horrible year like 2008, the banks replacing target bonuses with fully competitive salaries would have had far higher compensation expenses. We would have been spared the bold headlines about $18 billion in bonuses, but Wall Street's total compensation cost could easily have been another five or ten billion more than that."

Another well-intentioned governmental initiative contributed significantly to the ongoing difficulties for stockholders and boards of directors in adjusting executive compensation. As Robert Murphy writes, "The market has an elegant solution to bloated management who fritters away shareholder value: the corporate raider. Ironically, the government's restrictions on so-called hostile takeovers make it harder for shareholders in large corporations to clean house and install managers who will look out for their interests. As usual, the imperfections of the marketplace can be traced to the unintended consequences of earlier

"SHORT-TERMISM," NOT HIGH PAY, HELPED CAUSE THE CRISIS

The most trenchant analysis of the financial catastrophes of recent years suggests that businesses suffered more from their misguided basis for calculating executive rewards than from the mere size of bonuses and compensation packages. Judith Samuelson (of the Aspen Institute) and Lynn Stout (of UCLA Law School) summarized their conclusions in the *Wall Street Journal* (February 26, 2009): "Our economy didn't get into this mess because executives were paid too much. Rather, they were paid too much for doing the wrong things."

At the heart of the problem was "short-termism"—a tendency to emphasize quick, risky gains rather than steady, long-term progress. "Over the past decade, corporations in general—and banks and finance companies in particular—have become increasingly focused on a single, short-term goal: raising share price," write Samuelson and Stout. "Rather than focusing on producing quality products and services, they have become consumed with earnings management, 'financial engineering,' and moving risks off their balance sheets." The emphasis on stock options in executive compensation provided powerful incentives for the dangerous emphasis on short-term gain, since the value of the option depends exclusively on the price of the company's stock on the option exercise date—most often just a few years in the future.

Roy C. Smith of New York University, a former partner at Goldman Sachs, argues that merely lowering paychecks or bonuses will do nothing to change the perverse incentives built into the current system, but changing the emphasis on quick gain and short-term horizons must be a key element in any reform. "This needs to be fixed by increasing the proportion of bonuses that reflect performance over a longer term," he writes, "and to provide for 'clawbacks' of bonuses accrued when positions or transactions go awry at a later time. Many firms have begun to do this" (*Wall Street Journal*, February 7, 2009).

governmental interference." Roger Lowenstein of the *New York Times Magazine* (June 7, 2009) clearly agrees: "One positive effect of the hostile takeovers of the 1970s and '80s was to make CEOs aware that poor results would not be tolerated forever." With less threat of that sort of takeover, there is also less pressure to rein in free-spending executive indulgence.

REWARDING VIRTUE

In the face of abundant evidence that providing high executive pay, and even generous bonuses, will often make solid business sense, critics of the current compensation system tend to turn their attention from the companies that write the big checks to the corporate leaders who receive them. Regardless of the impact on the corporate bottom line, the argument goes, multimillion-dollar pay packages serve to corrupt and distract the very people they're meant to benefit. Psychoanalyst Kerry J. Sulkowicz wrote in *Business Week* (November 20, 2006) about the "psychology of CEO pay," urging that "we should also look at compensation's impact on a chief's personality and on his board relationships. Superstar pay can reinforce latent grandiose tendencies in those so predisposed." Dr. Sulkowicz cites a 2005 analysis by Washington University Law School professor Tony Paredes, who theorizes that "high pay can contribute to a CEO's overconfidence—in the face of which, board members are likely to be more deferential and less able to spot bad business decisions."

There is a long and honorable tradition, of course, behind the widespread fear that fabulous wealth will spoil the character and shatter the integrity of those who've achieved it. The Gospel According to Matthew (19:24) quotes the enigmatic declaration of Jesus that "it is easier for a camel to pass through the eye of a needle than for a rich man to enter the kingdom of heaven." The common understanding of this famous verse suggests that the accumulation of riches makes it less likely to achieve the spirit of humility, meekness, and kindness associated by Judeo-Christian tradition with godliness. The receipt of executive pay packages averaging more than $10 million a year can surely enhance a propensity to arrogance, a sense of entitlement, and isolation from ordinary folks who never fly in private planes, ride in limousines, receive elaborate plastic surgery, or ski at Gstaad. It's no accident that the most celebrated of all American films, *Citizen Kane,* portrays a visionary, hard-driving executive and entrepreneur who ends his life as a bitter, lonely old man, not in spite of the business empire he successfully constructed but because of it.

While there's never a shortage of baleful examples of business leaders who disgust the world with their rapacity, ruthlessness, or rudeness, it's worth noting that the free-market system punishes such appalling attributes far more often than rewarding them. On May 19, 2009, *New York Times* columnist David Brooks wrote a richly insightful piece about the traits most reliably associated with executive success. He cited a recently completed study called "Which CEO Characteristics and Abilities Matter?" by Steven Kaplan, Mark Klebanov, and Morten Sorensen. They compiled detailed personality assessments of 316 corporate chiefs and linked their personal qualities to the performance of their firms. "They found that strong people skills correlate loosely or not at all with being a good CEO. Traits like being a good listener, a good team builder, an enthusiastic colleague, a great communicator do not seem to be very important when it comes to leading successful companies."

What counted far more as a contributor to business success was an ability to focus—the disciplined, reliable, concentrated pursuit of clearly defined goals. As Brooks reports, "The traits that correlated most powerfully with success were attention to detail, persistence, efficiency, analytic thoroughness and the ability to work long hours. In other words, warm, flexible, team-oriented and empathetic people are less likely to thrive as CEOs. Organized, dogged, anal-retentive and slightly boring people are more likely to thrive."

The new study conformed closely to the conclusions from similar analysis of the ingredients for corporate success. *Good to Great,* a 2001 bestseller by Jim Collins, found that the top-performing chief executives were "humble, self-effacing, diligent and resolute souls who found one thing they were really good at and did it over and over again." That same year, Murray Barrick, Michael Mount, and Timothy Judge surveyed a hundred years of scientific analysis of business success. As Brooks describes it, they reported that what mattered most in scores of studies was "emotional stability, and, most of all, conscientious-

ness—which means being dependable, making plans and following through on them."

While Brooks never mentions it, the characteristics he delin-
eates as crucial for executive leadership read like traditional and
old-fashioned definitions of virtue. According to an abundance
of authoritative analysis, the corporate system rarely bestows its
highest honors on boisterous, erratic, or flamboyant behavior.
The lasting achievements stem from discipline, consistency, reliability, and the ability to defer gratification—the same qualities
that my grandmother (and many other grandmothers) tried to
encourage in the younger generation. For the corporate com-
mander, self-control will count more than salesmanship, and
concentration more than charisma.

Anyone who has already mastered such characteristics
should find an open road to business advancement. And anyone
who hasn't yet internalized these unabashedly bourgeois values
will see them implanted and encouraged as he seeks to climb
the corporate ladder. If, as is commonly assumed, the business
system will help shape personalities, then the natural selection process should discourage antisocial, disruptive, and destructive behavior and promote respectability and industriousness.
Rather than molding narcissistic frauds, experience in the free-
market economy should promote unassuming but dedicated
achievers who illustrate two of the most cherished aphorisms in
"Ethics of the Fathers," the most celebrated volume of the Talmud. There, rabbis from nearly two thousand years ago urged
their students to "say little and do much," and answered the
question "Who is mighty?" with the ringing declaration "He
who controls his own inclinations."

No wonder artistic personalities, with their emphasis on emo-
tion and spontaneity, feel no affinity for the world of business. As

Brooks concludes, "The virtues that writers tend to admire—those involving self-expression and self-exploration—are not the ones that lead to corporate excellence."

Rabbi Daniel Lapin emphasizes the inherently virtuous aspects of business success in his book *Thou Shall Prosper*. He writes that "deep within traditional Jewish culture lies the conviction that the only real way to achieve wealth is to attend diligently to the needs of others and conduct oneself in an honorable and trustworthy fashion. . . . The astounding news for the Jews was that God wants humans to be wealthy because wealth follows largely righteous conduct, which is His ultimate goal for His children."

Later, he counsels against the temptation of emphasizing a few deplorable examples—like the Bernie Madoffs of this world—to mischaracterize an overwhelmingly benign system of productivity and mutually beneficial relationships. "Conceding that [there are] many imperfections in the system that allows humans to cooperate economically," Lapin writes,

> is not the same as discrediting the entire enterprise of business, nor is it reason to do so. Yes, there have been many business professionals who have behaved scandalously. Business is a tool of human cooperation, and like any tool, it can be misused and abused. However, you should distinguish between judging certain conduct by business professionals as unethical and judging business itself. Only humans are capable of making moral decisions, and only humans can be judged and held accountable for those decisions and for the actions that flow from them. Like a sharp scalpel that can be used for healing in the hands of a dedicated surgeon or for assault in the hands of a thug, business can bring goodness and hope to all, or it can hurt.

In the long run, however, only one effort can ensure profitability and prosperity: reliably providing to others some good or service they need or want, and for which they are willing to pay with the fruits of their own labor. In this sense, every successful executive becomes a benefactor to his customers, as the free-market system compels service to your neighbor.

In a moving account for the popular children's magazine *Youth's Companion* in 1896, the great nineteenth-century steel baron and philanthropist Andrew Carnegie described his excitement upon bringing home his first week's pay for hard labor at the age of twelve. "I cannot tell you how proud I was when I received my first week's own earnings," he recalled. "One dollar and twenty cents made by myself and given to me because I had been of some use in the world! No longer entirely dependent on my parents, but at last admitted to the family partnership as a contributing member and able to help them! I think this makes a man out of a boy sooner than almost anything else, and a real man, too, if there be any germ of true manhood in him. *It is everything, to feel that you are useful"* (italics added).

This sense of usefulness, of service to a larger network of people, represents a richer reward for productive business activity than even the most lavish corporate pay package.

That's why business bashing usually falls flat when Americans have the chance to put the anticapitalist messages in context. In the midst of the presidential primaries of 2008, the widely admired former CEO of General Electric, Jack Welch (in collaboration with his wife, Suzy, former editor of the *Harvard Business Review*), responded this way to a demagogic Democrat from North Carolina who said, "For the past seven years, we've had a President who has stood up for corporations. It's time we had a President who stands up for you!":

ENCOURAGING CHARACTER, NOT CORRUPTION

Under the influence of lurid Hollywood imagery, many Americans harbor the mistaken idea that the best way to succeed in business is through double-dealing and utter ruthlessness, with no moral restraints on the personal or corporate behavior of aspiring captains of industry. Movies and TV shows regularly portray business leaders as equally reckless in the bedroom and the boardroom. Reality, on the other hand, far more conspicuously rewards restraint, concentration, and self-discipline, as most studies of economic success make clear. For instance, the *Wall Street Journal* recently posed a series of questions for budding business builders that would help determine their chances for success ("So, You Want to Be an Entrepreneur," February 23, 2009). The challenges listed—"Are you willing to sacrifice your lifestyle for potentially many years?" "Is your significant other on board?" "Are you a self-starter?" "Are you comfortable making decisions on the fly, with no playbook?"—focused almost entirely on questions of character and maturity rather than talent or resources.

Even in matters of intimate integrity, major corporations make far more rigorous demands on their leaders than the worlds of politics and media. During the Bill Clinton impeachment crisis of 1998–99, a common Republican mantra suggested that no corporate CEO could have survived revelations (and public lies) about a long-term dalliance with a youthful intern. In fact, less than six years later, the chief executive of one of the nation's largest companies lost his position because an investigation by the corporate board produced evidence of an affair. At Boeing, CEO Harry Stone-cipher (married and with grown children) resigned after ad-mitting a romantic involvement with a female executive. In less than three years (2003–05) Stonecipher's leadership had turned the company around, bringing an impressive 50 per-cent increase in the aircraft giant's stock price, but the board still demanded that he leave "because of actions inconsistent with Boeing's code of conduct, which reflected poorly on his judgment and would impair his ability to lead going forward." According to Cai von Rumohr, an analyst with SG Cowen Se-curities Corporation in Boston, "Under the circumstances, the person who heads Boeing has to be Mr. Clean. Basically the firing was done to restore the company's credibility. Performance-wise, the company was on an upswing. This will be yet another change, just when the company was starting to re-establish its momentum."

Governors, senators, and even a president of the United States (not to mention the most prominent figures in movies, television, and even broadcast journalism) have kept their ex-alted positions after behavior considerably more outrageous than Stonecipher's—suggesting that far from constituting a putrid sinkhole of corruption, most corporations continue to encourage (or even demand) some attention to traditional standards of decency.

"You, who?" the Welches asked. "Who are these 'you' people, we wonder, who aren't part of business in some way? Sure, some portion of the population is made up of students, government employees and workers in the nonprofit sector.

"But let's be real. The vast majority of Americans make their livelihoods from business, and not all of them are faceless, bloodless, megabonus-earning executives on Wall Street. They are the field workers of Big Oil, toiling in some of the harshest conditions on earth, from the oil sands of Canada to the high seas off the coast of Norway. They are the immunologists and oncologists of Big Pharma, hunkered down in their labs trying to find cures for AIDS and cancer.

"They are immigrants from Ecuador and Vietnam, running the restaurant around the corner or launching a high-tech venture in their garage. Our point is, corporations are not a bunch of buildings. Like all businesses, they are flesh and blood. They are human beings. And most of the time, they are human beings trying to make the world a better place for their families and employees. . . .

"Business isn't the enemy of people—it is people. And business doesn't destroy hope. It creates it."

THE HARPOONED WHALE

Which brings us back to the hopeless condition of onetime CEO Dennis Kozlowski, disgraced and imprisoned following the collapse of his high-flying career with Tyco. In his hauntingly poignant prison interview with Peter Hossli, Kozlowski continued to protest his innocence. "I think the jury got it wrong. I believe I earned those bonuses. I think I'm here simply because of the times. People lost money in the stock market in 2001 and 2002. Somebody had to be blamed for that. I became the poster boy for that. . . . In some years I made $100 million. I think having been tainted with that amount of money that the average person will say, 'Well, he must be doing something wrong.' That's why I was found guilty. . . .

"Nobody deserves $100 million," he continued, "no matter how good you are. But most of it came from stock appreciation. Our stock doubled every year for three or four years. I was paid about a million dollars to about a million five in cash. And everything else was earned through appreciation of the stock. I could have earned $100 million or I could have earned zero in the process."

Looking back on his obsessive pursuit of success, Kozlowski naturally regrets the lost time with his two daughters, and his single-minded commitment to the company he served for twenty-seven years. "I wanted to have Tyco become one of the best corporations in the world. I'm a competitive person and I enjoyed having Tyco rise above its peers. And I wanted to be a CEO who led Tyco to becoming one of the most prominent companies in the world."

After several years in his tiny jail cell in upstate New York, Kozlowski now realizes that he recklessly abused the conspicuous, surreal scale of his own prosperity, and foolishly abandoned the focused, results-oriented, self-effacing style of the CEOs with the best long-term records of success. "There is a saying that the only whale that gets harpooned is the one that comes up to the surface. I should have been content with far more modest growth in the company. With staying off of the radar, or returning shareholders a very reasonable rate of return and to be a more pedestrian CEO—doing a good job and then not trying to go out there and do a great job. So I don't think there were any rewards, only penalties associated with getting on everybody's radar and coming up to the surface."

In other words, he not only broke the law (according to the

jury that convicted him) but also violated the unwritten code of conduct that sustains more durable corporate leaders. He called attention to himself for all the wrong reasons, and even though his own company continued to prosper, Kozlowski's follies damaged the general reputation of business. Today, he appropriately regrets trading humility for hubris, corporate loyalty for faux fig wreaths. He says that he aspired to be great rather than merely good, but in the full glare of public resentment he ended his career by losing both greatness and goodness.

"Big Business Is Bad,
Small Business Is Good"

THE MOST POSITIVE FORCE IN OUR SOCIETY
VERSUS THE MOST MALEVOLENT

We Americans display a striking series of bizarre contradictions in our attitudes toward businesss—loving private companies when they're small and struggling but then suddenly hating them if they become too large and profitable. When asked about "big business," respondents in public opinion surveys react with fear, contempt, and resentment, associating the major enterprises that permeate every aspect of our lives with an array of vices and dangers. When it comes to "small business," however, we smile with warm approval, identifying these mom-and-pop operations with classic American values of hard work, decency, and neighborly concern. In overwhelming numbers, the public affirms the ludicrous notion that business contributes to progress and prosperity only so long as it achieves limited success.

A recent Harris poll (March 2007) reflected this schizophrenic approach to the free-market system. The pollsters asked respondents to assess their confidence level in the "people in charge of running" various institutions. "Small business" easily topped the poll, with 54 percent expressing a "great deal of confidence" in their leaders, and only 3 percent indicating "hardly any confidence at all." According to the survey, Americans look up to small business more than the military, the medical profession, organized religion, or any other segment of society. This raises an obvious question: if those who run small businesses truly deserve this sort of confidence, then why are their enterprises still small? The same survey, by the way, rated "major companies" near the bottom of the list (along with "organized labor" and "Congress"), with a scant 16 percent suggesting they felt a "great deal of confidence" in the big corporations that dominate our economy.

Many other polls produce similar results. In February 2009, Zogby International asked, "Who will lead us to a better future?" and "small business and entrepreneurs" led the way (with a resounding 63 percent), handily outpolling "government" (just 31 percent) and "large corporations and business leaders" (a meager 21 percent). Another Harris poll (March 2009) asked the public to classify those groups or institutions with "too much" or "too little" "power and influence in Washington, DC." Once again, "small business" placed at the very top of the list of fourteen categories, with an amazing 90 percent suggesting that these minor enterprises wielded "too little" influence. At the other extreme, "big companies" finished at rock bottom among the representative sample, with 85 percent declaring that they exerted "too much" power on the federal government.

In other words, for many—and perhaps even most—Americans, small business constitutes the most positive force in our society, while big business amounts to the most destructive and malevolent of all contemporary institutions. This stark dichotomy ignores the obvious reality that every big business began as a small enterprise, and every small business yearns to get big (or at least bigger).

Moreover, the polarized either/or reaction to insidious large companies versus admirable little firms ignores the obvious difficulty in determining what counts as a "big business." The official Department of Labor designation of small business involves those firms with fewer than 500 employees. Meanwhile, most recent statistics from the Small Business Administration show an impressive total of 4,857 enterprises with payrolls ranging from 400 employees to 499. Do these companies rightly count as lovable small businesses, or hateful big ones?

If a corporation's payroll inches up from 499 to 501 does it suddenly cease to serve its community and begin to menace the public interest? And what about the 8,974 firms that employ between 500 workers and 999? Do they properly deserve sympathy as plucky, virtuous small firms, or suspicion as predatory and arrogant corporate giants?

The illogical favoritism for little companies over big ones, for minor firms struggling for survival over the nation's most major, well-established, and prodigiously prosperous enterprises, owes a great deal to the instinctive, deep-rooted American preference for the underdog. Americans love upsets and upstarts: we reflexively root for David, not Goliath, and only a strange breed (mostly within New York's five boroughs) chooses to vote for the wealthy, free-spending, predictably formidable Yankees.

FIGHTING THE "MONEY POWER"

A sentimental preference for minor, unassuming, local endeavors dates from the earliest days of the Republic and arose in part from unique historical circumstances. Colonial settlements and frontier outposts struggled for survival, as pioneers confronted loneliness, deprivation, and danger with few of the comforts and options of established cities. In this context, the opening of a new general store (or tavern, or blacksmith, or apothecary, or cobbler) amounted to such an obvious boon to a raw, tenuous community that no one worried about the new merchant's pursuit of profit, or fretted over the chance that he'd enrich himself at the expense of his neighbors. If, on the other hand, a subsistence farmer purchased a new plow from some distant, faceless company "back East," the resentment at paying off the outrageous cost of even the most necessary implement overrode any sense of feeling blessed by its availability. The unprecedented distances in the vast new nation helped to shape the powerful distinction between good small businesses (our friends and neighbors) and evil big firms (our faraway class enemies). For several centuries, the distrust of big business was connected to feelings of alienation by the nation's agrarian majority from the commercial interests in remote urban centers (or even Europe).

In one of the most famous (and stirring) expressions of that distrust, a thirty-six-year-old Nebraska lawyer who had served briefly in Congress addressed the Democratic National Convention in 1896. "You come to us and tell us that the great cities are in favor of the gold standard," said William Jennings Bryan. "We reply that the great cities rest upon our broad and fertile prairies. Burn down your cities and leave our farms, and your cities will spring up again as if by magic; but destroy our farms and the grass will grow in the streets of every city of the country." The delegates in Chicago went wild when the "Boy Orator of the Platte" framed the choice in the upcoming election as "a struggle between the idle holders of idle capital and the struggling masses, who produce the wealth and pay the taxes of the country." The idea that "idle capital" played a necessary role in funding the business enterprises that allowed the "struggling masses" to produce that wealth never troubled the delirious Democrats, who proceeded to shock the world by nominating the unknown from Omaha for the first of his three (unsuccessful) presidential bids.

For Bryan (and the populists who preceded and inspired him), the prairie farmer toiling day and night to produce and sell his crops constituted the prime example of the virtuous small businessman, while city slicker bankers or factory owners, with their mysterious manipulation of money, represented the vile corruption of big business. A hundred years earlier, Thomas Jefferson had emphasized the same distinctions while similarly idealizing the humble souls who tilled the soil. At a time when the biggest towns in the country (including Philadelphia, New

ANDREW JACKSON: CONSERVATIVE STALWART, NOT POPULIST BUSINESS-BASHER

Liberal Democrats of the twenty-first century have frequently claimed Andrew Jackson as one of their historical heroes, comparing his battles on behalf of "the common man" and against "big business" to the bold governmental activism of Barack Obama. This identification helped to make a triumphal bestseller out of an admiring 2008 biography (*American Lion: Andrew Jackson in the White House*) by outspokenly progressive *Newsweek* editor Jon Meacham. Much to the disappointment of doctrinaire leftists, however, Meacham's readable account makes clear that Jackson's impassioned denunciations of "the Money Power" actually centered on his fears of government's corrupting entanglement with business, not on the free development of corporations in the largely unfettered economy of his day. The seventh president's Farewell Address, in fact, unmistakably echoes timeless conservative (or libertarian) themes: "There is but one safe rule, and that is to confine the General Government rigidly within the sphere of its appropriate duties. It has no power to raise a revenue or impose taxes except for the purposes enumerated in the Constitution, and if its income is found to exceed these wants it should be forthwith reduced and the burden of the people so far lightened."

Jackson's minimalist approach to government led to his impassioned, obsessive abhorrence of the national debt. He inherited a debt of $48,565,000 when he moved into the White House in 1829, having previously described this burden as a "national curse." A year later he told Congressman (and future vice president) Richard M. Johnson of Kentucky, "I stand committed before the country to pay off the national debt at the earliest practicable moment. This pledge I am determined to redeem." To accomplish that redemption, the president vetoed legislation for popular road-building projects on the sensible ground that the Treasury contained no money to pay for them. After six years of tightfisted leadership, Jackson proudly announced that the nation would be debt-free as of January 1, 1835, with a balance on hand of $440,000. To celebrate this signal achievement, a Washington dinner commemorated Old Hickory's triumph over debt combined with the twentieth anniversary of his great battlefield victory at New Orleans. "The national debt is paid!" exulted Senator Thomas Hart Benton in a toast, marking Jackson's success as "resplendent, glorious and beneficent for his country." Former treasury secretary (and future chief justice) Roger B. Taney crowed that it was "the first time in the history of nations that a large public debt has been entirely extinguished." As John Steele Gordon noted in 2004, "It remains the only time to this day." Certainly, no one expects President Obama (with an annual deficit approaching $2 trillion and a national debt of nearly $12 trillion—$12,000,000,000,000) to emulate the achievement of his Democratic predecessor.

York, and Boston) amounted to little more than overgrown villages with barely 50,000 inhabitants, Jefferson still characterized cities as "ulcers on the body politic. In the words of economic historian John Steele Gordon, the third president nurtured a vision of America as "a land of self-sufficient yeoman farmers, a rural utopia that never really existed and would be utterly at odds with the American economy as it actually developed in the industrial age then just coming into being." Jefferson loathed the rude, moneygrubbing spirit of Philadelphia, or London, for that matter; during the worldwide struggle between Britain and France that haunted his presidency he tilted in a French direction in part because he shared Napoleon's contempt for the English as "a nation of shopkeepers." As a child of inherited privilege (the death of his father left him more than 5,000 acres of land and 300 slaves), he could afford disdain for the "getting and spending" poetically reviled by his contemporary Wordsworth; despite all the hundreds of laborers who toiled for him in the fields and shops around Monticello, it seemed never to occur to him that he himself ran a big business. He expressed his disdain for commercial values with a lifelong habit of self-destructive spending and thoughtless borrowing, leaving behind a mountain of unpaid (and largely ignored, unsecured) debts when he died at age eighty-three. "I have ever been the enemy of banks," he wrote to his friend (and former rival) John Adams in old age. "My zeal against these institutions was so warm and open at the establishment of the Bank of the U.S. that I was derided as a Maniac by the tribe of bank-mongers, who were seeking to filch from the public their swindling, and barren gains."

The "bank-mongers," led by Jefferson's rival Alexander Hamilton, decisively triumphed in that fateful battle within the Washington administration, setting up the First Bank of the United States and lending much-needed financial stability to the early years of the Republic. In 1811, a sharply divided Congress failed to recharter the central bank (when Madison's vice president, George Clinton, broke a tie vote in the Senate), but five years later the skeptics reconsidered. The funding and financial struggles associated with the War of 1812 persuaded President Madison, despite his impeccable Jeffersonian credentials, that the nation needed an official, dominant bank—the ultimate big business.

The Second Bank of the United States made major contributions to the Republic's spectacular growth in the years that followed, and President Andrew Jackson's implacable hatred of the institution stemmed more from its political influence than its economic operations. Jackson introduced some of the most persistent and persuasive objections to big business in his bitter war against the bank, which he scowlingly described as "the Money Power." The president warned that the concentration of such great wealth and influence in an institution operated for private gain threatened to distort the operations of government. In vetoing a new charter for the Bank of the United States in 1832, his most celebrated objection declared, "It is to be regretted that the rich and powerful too often bend the acts of government to their selfish purposes. Distinctions in society will always exist under every just government. Equality of talents, of education, or of wealth can not be produced by human institutions. In the full enjoyment of the gifts of Heaven and the fruits of superior industry, economy, and virtue, every man is equally entitled to protection by law but when the laws undertake to add to these natural and just advantages artificial distinctions, to grant titles, gratuities, and exclusive privileges, to make the rich richer and potent more powerful, the humble members of society—the farmers, mechanics, and laborers—who have neither the time nor the means of securing like favors to themselves, have a right to complain of the injustice of their Government."

Unlike Jefferson, Jackson didn't see himself as an enemy of banks in general, but only of a single, huge financial institution that wielded its power through government favor and sponsorship. After killing the effort to recharter the Bank of the United States, Old Hickory removed federal funds and placed them instead in an array of lesser state banks. These "pet banks" of the Jackson administration seemed more worthy and less menacing precisely because they were smaller. With the blessing of the government, minor financial institutions sprang up everywhere; the number of banks in the country more than doubled from 329 in 1829 to 788 in 1837. In the absence of the steadying influence of a central bank, speculation exploded and then crashed.

In a matter of months, some 343 banks failed entirely; 62 failed partially. By early fall of 1837 (under the new president, Martin Van Buren), 90 percent of the nation's factories had closed and unemployment, not yet officially calculated by government, rose to previously unimagined levels. Best estimates suggest that more than one in four laborers failed to find work, and federal revenues instantly fell by half. The depression lasted a full seventy-two months and thoroughly shattered confidence in the American business system. John Steele Gordon points to a telling passage in Charles Dickens's international bestseller *A Christmas Carol* (1843): when Ebenezer Scrooge realizes that a note payable to him may yet be redeemed, he's relieved to see that it's not as worthless as "a mere United States' security."

The hatred of big business assumed new forms following the nation's slow recovery from the Panic of 1837. Jacksonians feared that a handful of huge enterprises would "bend the acts of government to their selfish ends"; they worried, ultimately, about the abuse of political, not economic, power. According to

Alan Greenspan in 1961 (yes, *that* Alan Greenspan—future chairman of the Federal Reserve), "Americans have always feared the concentration of arbitrary power in the hands of politicians. Prior to the Civil War, few attributed such power to businessmen. It was recognized that government officials had the legal power to compel obedience by the use of physical force—and that businessmen had no such power. A businessman needed customers. He had to appeal to their self interest."

"THE CURSE OF BIGNESS"

After the War Between the States, the rapid rise of national railroads and other major corporations radically altered public perceptions. Residents in the well-settled Eastern states could choose from any number of competing and established rail lines that crisscrossed their territory, but vast stretches of the thinly populated West and upper Midwest relied on a single set of tracks and a single company. These corporations dramatically expanded with federal approval and, to some extent, governmental sponsorship following the Civil War. Federal leaders wanted to unify the recently divided nation with "bands of steel"—railroad tracks linking every corner of the vast continent—but the resulting business behemoths, with their limitless scope and uncontested authority, terrified the hard-pressed tillers of the soil. As Greenspan noted in his fascinating essay "Antitrust": "Outwardly, the railroads did not have the backing of legal force. But to the farmers of the West, the railroads seemed to hold arbitrary power previously ascribed solely to government."

The situation led to desperate demands for federal and state action to cut the largest companies down to size and to return them to local control, with the forlorn hope that such antibusiness intervention could foster competition and benefit the public. In place of the strict governmental neutrality envisioned by Jefferson and Jackson, the bashers of big business now wanted aggressive federal and state intrusion to curb "unhealthy" corporate growth. Previous critics of powerful companies worried that those corporations would partner with government to oppress the people; now the self-proclaimed champions of the common man wanted ordinary people to partner with government to tame the corporations.

This agitation led directly to the Interstate Commerce Act of 1887 and, three years later, to passage of the Sherman Antitrust Act to outlaw "combinations in restraint of trade" and to threaten jail terms for any and all who sought monopolistic control. Drafted by Ohio's GOP senator John Sherman (a perennial presidential candidate and older brother of Civil War hero William Tecumseh Sherman), the legislation won near-unanimous approval despite the domination of both houses of Congress by purportedly pro-business Republicans.

The Sherman Act enshrined as government policy the peculiar idea that any business combination efficient and successful enough to dominate its market niche deserved suspicious scrutiny, if not outright punishment, by federal authorities. Some fifty-eight years after the law's passage, Supreme Court Justice William O. Douglas explicitly interpreted the purpose of the legislation as a curb on the size and scope of corporations, rather than a ban of specific business practices. "We have here the problem of bigness," he wrote in a dissenting opinion in the antitrust action *United States v. Columbia Steel Co.* "The Curse of Bigness shows how size can become a menace—both industrial and social. It can be an industrial menace because it creates gross inequalities against existing or putative competitors." In other words, Justice Douglas wanted governmental intervention on the side of small, weak, struggling competitors that might not otherwise survive against a thriving capitalist concern. "Industrial power should be decentralized," he declared. "It should be scattered into many hands so that the fortunes of the people will not be dependent on the whim or caprice, the political prejudices, the emotional stability of a few self-appointed men. . . . That is the philosophy and the command of the Sherman Act. It is founded on a theory of hostility to the concentration in private hands of power so great that only a government of the people should have it." In other words, the extent of corporate growth and development should be detemined by judges, bureaucrats, and politicians, not the dynamics of the marketplace.

ANTITRUST INSANITY

At the beginning of the twentieth century, President Theodore Roosevelt won enthusiastic public support for his well-publicized "trust-busting" under the Sherman Act, launching forty-five lawsuits against private companies. His conservative successor, William Howard Taft, pursued antitrust cases even more vigorously, with seventy-five pieces of major litigation in his single term (1909–13). A hundred years later the efforts to dispel "the Curse of Bigness" have metastasized into a vast, swollen bureaucracy: according to 2009 figures, the Antitrust Division of the Department of Justice employs a full-time staff of 773, at an annual cost to taxpayers of $150,591,000 (an increase of more than 34 percent since 2000).

This investment has purchased such legal travesties as the hugely complex and costly litigation against Microsoft by the Department of Justice and twenty states beginning in 1998. The feds pounced on the software giant not for gouging the public with high prices but for bundling its Internet Explorer web browser at no additional charge together with its ubiquitous Windows operating system. The company and its supporters counterattacked in the court of public opinion, with a newspaper ad signed by 240 economists that declared, "Consumers did not ask for these antitrust actions—rival business firms did. Consumers of high technology have enjoyed falling prices, expanding outputs, and a breathtaking array of new products and innovations. . . . Increasingly, however, some firms have sought to handicap their rivals by turning to government for protection. Many of these cases are based on speculation about some vaguely specified consumer harm in some unspecified future, and many of the proposed interventions will weaken successful U.S. firms and impede their competitiveness abroad."

Despite this logic, the trial judge ordered Microsoft split in two as punishment for its consumer-friendly misdeeds, and during the appeal process the company agreed to a settlement that terminated some of the practices specifically challenged by the government—even though Bill Gates insisted that efficiency would suffer in the process. Meanwhile, the Netscape browser, which the federal lawsuit specifically aimed to protect, still failed to hold its own in a hugely competitive arena, falling to less than 1 percent of the market before its virtual disappearance and purchase by AOL. Eight years after the bitter litigation came to an end, Microsoft's Internet Explorer still draws 65.5 percent of all browser users but faces robust competition from Mozilla Firefox and Safari (rivals that played little or no role in the lawsuits), as well as a daunting new challenge from Google Chrome.

Previous antitrust prosecutions in the computer industry proved similarly misguided and ineffectual—in particular the bloody thirteen-year battle against a respected corporate innovator that once dominated the field. As John Steele Gordon recalled in *Forbes* magazine: "Go back to 1969. The Microsoft of the day was the International Business Machine Corp.—seemingly invincible, with a 65 percent share of the computer market. The little guys were being squashed. Burroughs, Sperry, General Electric, Honeywell, Control Data. More, perhaps, to protect them than to protect consumers, the U.S. government sued IBM, demanding that the company be dismantled." In other words, federal power intervened unapologetically in a competitive industry to support smaller companies and to damage their more successful rival. Even at the time, no one claimed that attacking IBM would produce direct, immediate benefit to the public in terms of lower prices or better products. As Gordon concludes, "By the time the Justice Department dropped the case in 1982, mainframes had begun a long, slow fade from glory. Before the decade was over, IBM was heading into serious trouble and was soon to lay off thousands of employees."

Gordon also associates antitrust policies with the inexorable, tragic decline of one of the nation's greatest companies. "General Motors never suffered a government antitrust attack, but lived for years in holy terror of one," he writes. Gordon goes on to cite Alfred D. Chandler, the Pulitzer Prize–winning business historian at Harvard, who recalled conversations with Alfred P. Sloan, GM's chairman during its glory years, from 1937 to 1956. "Sloan knew that if GM topped 45 percent in market share it would have an antitrust problem, but telling his managers to stop at 45 percent was telling them not to work hard. And Sloan was right. American automobile technology and manufacturing largely went to sleep in the postwar years." Gordon made these observations in 1998, a full decade before Detroit finally awoke from that long slumber with the GM bankruptcy that shocked the world. Destructive government policy that once discouraged General Motors from becoming too large, too prosperous, too dominant now gave way to expensive government intervention to prevent the company from disappearing altogether.

History demonstrates that even without the fear of aggressive antitrust assaults by government, control of any major industry by a single company proves ephemeral. With the U.S. economy presenting few insurmountable barriers to entry, fresh competitors—frequently deploying fresh technologies—can challenge even the most formidably established industry leaders. As Alan Greenspan describes the normal pattern of industrial development and market maturation, "An industry begins with a few small firms; in time, many of them merge; this increases efficiency and augments profits. As the market expands, new firms enter the field, thus cutting down the share of the market held by the dominant firm. This has been the pattern in steel, oil, aluminum, containers, and numerous other major industries. The observable tendency of an industry's dominant companies eventually to lose part of their share of the market is not caused by antitrust legislation, but by the fact that it is difficult to prevent new firms from entering the field when the demand for a certain product increases. Texaco and Gulf, for example, would have grown into large firms even if the original Standard Oil Trust had not been dissolved."

Once hailed as an economic genius and the all-knowing "Maestro" who orchestrated a record-setting boom, now reviled as a bumbling manipulator whose ill-advised decisions contributed to financial collapse, Alan Greenspan the Fed chairman has become a deeply controversial figure. But his observations and analysis in "Antitrust" (originally published as part of the 1961 Ayn Rand anthology *Capitalism: The Unknown Ideal*) remain unassailable.

"The world of antitrust is reminiscent of Alice's Wonderland," he writes. "It is a world in which competition is lauded as the basic axiom and guiding principle, yet 'too much' competition is condemned as 'cutthroat.' It is a world in which actions designed to limit competition are branded as criminal when taken by businesses, yet praised as 'enlightened' when initiated by government. It is a world in which the law is so vague that businessmen have no way of knowing whether specific actions will be declared illegal until they hear the judge's verdict—after the fact."

He concludes that accused "monopolists" actually merit recognition for nurturing and enlarging their enterprises and steering them to the commanding positions that drew government attention in the first place: "It takes extraordinary skill to hold more than fifty percent of a large industry's market in a free economy. It requires unusual productive ability, unfailing business judgment, unrelenting effort at the continuous improvement of one's product and technique. The rare company which is able to retain its share of the market year after year and decade after decade does so by means of productive efficiency—and deserves praise, not condemnation."

GLOBALIZATION AND ITS DISCONTENTS

The same envious instinct to strike out against any enterprise guilty of achieving supremacy in the marketplace drives the

"EVERYONE AGREES. IT'S ABOUT TO EXPLODE"

Despite the severe dislocations of the economic crisis, the fanatical antiglobalization movement became less visible after the intensive publicity surrounding the "Battle in Seattle." Most recently, the anarchist and antimaterialist fringe has focused on publishing anonymous manifestos and random acts of sabotage rather than mass demonstrations. In 2007, a shadowy French group known only as "The Invisible Committee" published a controversial volume confidently entitled *The Coming Insurrection.* The opening lines of this literary salvo—"Everyone agrees. It's about to explode"—became a rallying cry for deeply alienated youth in Europe. "The economy is itself the crisis," the unidentified authors declared. "It's not that there's not enough work, it's that there's too much of it." They deplored a "diseased and dehumanizing civilization that cannot be reformed" and instead must be "torn apart and replaced." To achieve those goals, The Invisible Committee called upon readers to "sabotage authority," to form self-sufficient communes, and to join "a conspiracy against commodity society." In 2008, French police arrested nine radicals who shared a farmhouse near Tarnac and charged them with an attack on railroad power lines that disabled 160 trains, stranding 40,000 passengers for six hours on November 8. The authorities and the press identified the saboteurs as the authors of *The Coming Insurrection,* which appeared in the United States in an English translation in June 2009. Despite the book's explosive rhetoric (with deliberate echoes of the "final conflict" heralded more than a century earlier by "The Internationale"), its publication produced neither insurrection nor robust sales in the United States.

hysterical opposition to the inevitable next stage for most American companies: expansion into the international arena. The fear that a business might grow so big that it exerts dangerous power over one industry, or even over one nation, has given way to darker terrors of global, transnational dominance. Critics of globalization rally wherever financial and diplomatic leaders gather to promote international trade, and the protestors stage angry demonstrations, complete with huge papier-mâché effigies of various "corporate criminals."

These anticapitalist carnivals regularly degenerate into nasty riots, like 1999's bloody and destructive "Battle in Seattle," which erupted just a block from my office and a few miles from my home. Some forty thousand demonstrators converged on the ministerial meeting of the World Trade Organization at the Washington State Convention Center just a few weeks before Christmas and proceeded to express their idealism by trashing the traditional Santa Claus Lane that had been set up for the children of the city at Nordstrom's department store. Anarchists in black ski masks also showed their rage at big business by shattering windows and smashing equipment at the Starbucks across the street from my office. While the parent company certainly could be classified as a large, international corporation, it apparently never occurred to the antiglobalist thugs that the neighborhood operation that suffered the brunt of their attack functioned for its regular customers and employees as a classic small businessman. Other shopkeepers faced down the invaders on their own: the proprietor of a family-owned jewelry store (and a decorated veteran of the Israeli army) stood in his doorway with a baseball bat and effectively fought off dozens of rioters, without waiting for the overtaxed cops (who were busy a few blocks away arresting six hundred demonstrators). The

NO EXCEPTIONS TO UNBREAKABLE RULES

In fact, the expansion of U.S. corporations overseas has brought enormous benefits to both America and our trading partners. Scott Davis, chairman and CEO of United Parcel Service (another company that happened to originate in the Seattle area, coincidentally), defended international commerce in the *Wall Street Journal* (July 14, 2009), noting that "growth in trade since World War II has added an average of about *$1 trillion* a year to America's income (in 2003 dollars) according to economists at the Peter G. Peterson Institute for International Economics. . . . Trade actually generates jobs. The United States is the world's largest exporter of goods and services. Its total exports last year reached $1.8 trillion. The Treasury Department estimates that as many as 57 million Americans work for companies enaged in global commerce."

These American gains hardly come at the expense of others. Like most reasonable business transactions, the development of international trade has helped all participants— particularly the huge nations that formerly held the biggest share of the world's poor. In April 2007, Robyn Meredith and Suzanne Hoppough concluded in *Forbes* magazine, "It turns out that globalization is good—and not just for the rich, but especially for the poor. The booming economies of India and China—the Elephant and the Dragon—have lifted 200 million people out of abject poverty in the 1990's as globalization took off, the International Monetary Fund says. . . . In the next eight years almost 1 billion people across Asia will take a Great Leap Forward into a new middle class. In China, middle-class incomes are set to rise threefold, to $5,000 predicts Dominic Barton, a Shanghai managing partner for McKinsey & Co. As the Chindia revolution spreads, the ranks of the poor get smaller, not larger."

The only nations that remained untouched by the world-wide progress were those that deliberately excluded themselves from the increasingly dynamic global economy—with North Korea and Cuba, in their ascetic Communist purity, offering particularly depressing and isolated examples. Fareed Zakaria of *Newsweek* and CNN observed in the *New York Times* (May 1, 2005), "You cannot switch off these forces except at great cost to your own economic well-being. Over the last century, those countries that tried to preserve their systems, jobs, culture or traditions by keeping the rest of the world out all stagnated. Those that opened themselves to the world prospered." At both extremes, recent history provides no exceptions to these unbreakable rules.

high-spirited protestors couldn't possibly have mistaken the tiny jeweler for a multinational powerhouse; the store seemed to represent precisely the sort of local, small-gauge, grandpa-and-grandma enterprise that antiglobalists say they support. But they tried to ransack the place nonetheless.

Such contradictions never trouble the ferocious foes of globalization, who proudly unite demagogues of both the extreme Left and the extreme Right. Three-time presidential candidate Pat Buchanan (a longtime critic of free trade) turned up in Seattle and made common cause with environmental extremists in sea turtle costumes, solemnly marching socialist trade unionists, and anarchist taggers with black scarves who decorated down-town buildings with their crudely spray-painted "circle A" symbol. Most of the protestors hated international trade because it allegedly enriched America at the expense of the developing world, while Pitchfork Pat denounced multinational deals because they purportedly impoverished America for the sake of other nations. When I interviewed leaders of "the resistance" on my radio show, they remained deeply confused and conflicted over who suffered and who benefited from the commerce they decried, but energetically agreed that corporate growth across international boundaries amounted to an unalloyed and menacing evil. Once again, they associated the idea of companies getting big with the prospect of them going bad.

ENRICHED, NOT ENDANGERED

Nevertheless, some activists and politicians in every nation try to keep out foreign companies, motivated as much by cultural as economic fears. For years, our erstwhile allies, the French, fretted that Mickey Mouse and Big Macs would overwhelm and pollute their vastly more refined culture and they promulgated numerous regulations to restrict the degrading influence of Uncle Sam. Nevertheless, after seventeen years of Euro Disney (where, in deference to local custom, all seven dwarves are named "Grumpy"), and after a generation of McDonald's, Paris is still Paris, sophisticated gourmands maintain their unaccountable lust for snails, and French tastes in general remain the world's snootiest and most distinctive. Fears of imposed, uniform corporate or cultural hegemony by crude, clumsy, invading Americans had been hugely overblown; the introduction of overseas alternatives provided additional elements without subtracting anything from the Parisian mix.

For those who assume that globalization will undermine cultural diversity, Richard D. McCormick, retired CEO of US West, makes a valuable suggestion. "Get on the internet and type 'blankets' or 'jewelry' or 'sculpture' or 'food,'" he told a 2000 audience at the Denver World Trade Center. "You'll discover, as thousands of 'bootstrap' business and crafts people around the world have—globalization expands diversity. It gives geographically isolated crafts-people a worldwide market for their goods and services. It does the same for dances, and dramas. Religions. Political philosophies. And shared interests as well.

"Yes, it filled our living rooms with Asian made stereos and TVs. But most of us still play American music and programs.

"Yes, globalization brought McDonald's to Hong Kong. But the menu there has had to take on a decidedly Asian flavor, as well as giving Asians a new choice. We get new choices, too. And, most of the time, we like them. . . . Diversity is not endangered by globalization—it's enriched."

This means that when big U.S. corporations begin to operate internationally, they become less dominant, not more so. Justice Douglas's fears about "the curse of bigness" begin to evaporate when companies become big enough to operate beyond national borders and engage a raft of aggressive (and often impressive) new competitors. In July 2000, professors Pankaj Ghemawat and Fariborz Ghadar wrote in the *Harvard Business Review* of the mistaken "common wisdom" that "industries will become more concentrated as they become more global." They "debunk the myth of increased concentration; the perceived

"A TALE OF TWO CONTINENTS"

The best way to assess the impact of globalization and free trade is to compare the progress of those societies that welcomed international commerce with those that resisted it. In his 2004 book *In Defense of Globalization,* Columbia professor Jagdish Bhagwati contrasts the pace of development in Asia and Africa. As recently as 1970, average incomes in Africa were 30 percent higher than average Asian incomes. Thirty years later, incomes in Africa remained stagnant—and amounted to less than half of their Asian counterparts. While acknowledging many contributing factors in this dramatic reversal, Bhagwati cites as primary cause the fact that "Asia opened itself and adapted to external markets while Africa did not." As a result, the world center of poverty shifted: In 1970, Asia was home to 75 percent of the world's poor, and Africa only 10 percent, using United Nations standard measures of absolute poverty. By 2000, more than a third of the world's poor lived in Africa, and just 15 percent in Asia. As Bhagwati concludes, trade and foreign direct investment boost growth, and growth reduces poverty.

links between the globalization of an industry and the concentration of that industry are weak. Empirical research shows that global—or globalizing—industries have actually been marked by steady decreases in concentration since World War II." They also reported that "the oil industry is actually far less concentrated today than it was 50 years ago, with more than 20 equal-sized competitors in the field today. . . . Analysis of industries such as zinc, bauxite and copper also reveals decreased global concentration since World War II. . . . GM, Ford and Toyota together control less of the world's car market today than GM alone controlled in 1950."

This means that consumers enjoy more choice than ever before, as the situation with automobiles dramatically demonstrates. When I was a boy in the remote 1950s and '60s, buying a car used to involve just two basic decisions for my dad: first, which of the Big Three Detroit companies he selected, and second, which model within the chosen corporate universe (usually Ford) he wanted to buy. Today, in contrast, automotive shoppers confront a dazzling array of exotic alternatives, from lumbering Hummers and Land Rovers to petite, zippy Smart Cars and Mini Coopers, some of them involving imported brands with names (Hyundai? Kia? Subaru?) unknown to earlier generations. In the immediate future, new low-cost imports from India and China will, apparently, expand available options even further, with the sheer variety of vehicles (including hybrids and electrics) unimaginable without international trade. If you're a car company executive or an auto worker in Detroit, you may rightly resent this situation, but if you're a potential car buyer you ought to celebrate it—especially because that new car will cost a smaller percentage of the typical household's annual income than your parents or grandparents paid. An average new car in 1950 (without air-conditioning, of course, or FM radio, CD player, power windows, cruise control, and other familiar present-day frills) cost 24.4 weeks of the normal family's income. In 2008, a typical new vehicle (with hugely enhanced technological sophistication) required 21.5 weeks of household income to cover its cost.

MAKING NECESSITIES
AND LUXURIES MORE AFFORDABLE

Far from imposing the price gouging, exploitation, and other forms of corporate bullying predicted by angry anticapitalist protestors, the globalization process has made both necessities and luxuries more affordable. Transnational enterprises, instead of wiping out local companies in the developing world, provide the goods and services that can make them more productive—and more capable of satisfying the intensified demand that always accompanies rapidly rising standards of living. As Richard D. McCormick points out, "Globalization and freer trade make market access easier for everyone—especially small businesses, which are quick to adopt new technologies. The big winners, of course, are consumers. As companies—big and small—compete, consumers get more choices and better prices. Price increases for global products—the cars, computers and stereos—are smaller than those for local products and services, like haircuts and houses." He cites a study by the Organisation for Economic Co-operation and Development showing that from 1980 to 1995 consumer prices in the OECD countries rose overall by 175 percent. Meanwhile, the cost of internationally traded goods—the "world trade stuff"—rose by only 40 percent.

In the United States, nearly everyone understands that the importation of foreign goods (particularly from China) helps eager consumers save a great deal of money at Walmart (and elsewhere). The same dynamic operates nearly everywhere around the world, with a larger selection and more competition reliably delivering lower prices.

It's only logical that when more products arrive to compete

for the same consumer dollars, lower prices will result. By the same token, the phenomenon of more employers competing for the same workers will produce higher wages. If an overseas company comes to town in Bangkok or Buenos Aires, the boss won't secure the workforce he needs by offering less money than the prevailing wage. To get capable, productive employees to join a newly arrived international firm, it's normal to offer more, not less, in the pay envelopes. In fact, the 2000 study by the OECD found that foreign corporations pay more than the average wage *in every country in which they operate.* Without exception, international enterprises benefited rather than blighted local workers. In Turkey, for example, foreign companies paid a full 24 percent more than the national average.

In America, the same dynamic delivers higher-than-usual compensation for domestic employees of foreign-owned firms. In a 2004 paper for the National Center for Policy Analysis, former Reagan aide Bruce Bartlett noted that "insourced jobs"—positions in overseas businesses operating within the United States—"pay 16.5 percent more than the average domestic job, and one third of them are in the manufacturing sector. These include plants that assemble German and Japanese automobiles and produce pharmaceuticals."

While politicians and TV commentators rail against "outsourcing"—the purchase of services for American companies that are performed by workers abroad—the welcome occurrence of insourcing actually plays an even larger role in the U.S. economy. For instance, Senator John Kerry ran for president in 2004 with daily denunciations of "Benedict Arnold CEOs or companies who ship the jobs overseas and stick Americans with the bill" (Manchester, New Hampshire, January 27, 2004). The Democratic nominee might have spoiled his stump speech by acknowledging that even as he spoke, Americans got far more jobs from foreign companies than U.S. companies provided for workers abroad. Daniel Griswold, director of the Center for Trade Policy Studies at the Cato Institute, prepared a report (September 2004) showing that Americans "by far and away" led the world in completing work for foreign corporations, primarily with "information technology, financial, communications and other business services." In 2003, Americans sold $131 billion in private business services to the rest of the world. Those services include such outsourcing tasks as legal work, computer programming, management consulting, telecommunications, banking, and engineering. At the same time, Americans were buying or importing $77 billion worth of business services from the rest of the world, including call center and data-entry services from developing countries such as India and the Philippines. In other words, when it comes to outsourcing of business services, the United States ran a $54 billion surplus with the rest of the world.

This means, when companies (both domestic and foreign) get bigger through expansion of their international operations, that growth is more likely to enrich rather than impoverish Americans. Matthew J. Slaughter, associate dean of the Tuck School of Business at Dartmouth, recently observed in the *Wall Street Journal* (May 7, 2009) that "it is important to understand that America today has a robust automobile industry thanks to insourcing. In 2006, foreign-headquartered multinationals engaged in making and wholesaling motor vehicles and parts employed 402,800 Americans—at an average annual compensation of $63,538—20 percent above the national average. Amid the Big Three struggles of the past generation, insourcing companies like Toyota, Honda and Mercedes have greatly expanded automobile operations in the U.S. In fiscal year 2008, Toyota assembled 1.66 million motor vehicles in North America with production in seven U.S. states supported by research and development in three more.... And it means that some of the best companies in America are foreign-owned insourcing companies."

Slaughter went on to note the enormously positive impact of large, international enterprises on United States workers and consumers. "Today, insourcing companies strengthen America's economy across all industries. In 2006, they employed more than 5.3 million Americans, conducted $34.3 billion in research and development, invested $160.2 billion in capital, and exported $195.3 billion in goods. If Chrysler partners with Italy's Fiat as the president hopes, it will join the ranks of these insourcing companies.... Chrysler and GM will be stronger if they can become more global, not less so. This should benefit not just their bottom lines but their U.S. workers. Much research now shows that expansion abroad by U.S. companies tends to support jobs in America, not destroy them."

CONTRARY TO WIDESPREAD PERCEPTIONS

While ignoring this research, antitrade true believers regularly cite three factors to support their conviction that international commerce (conducted by big businesses grown to global scale) actually damages the United States and the world at large:

1. the sharp decline in the number of manufacturing jobs in America
2. the alarming and relentless increase in the nation's trade deficit

3. the potential of environmental devastation as United States businesses expand abroad

Each of these objections deserves a direct, logical, and brief rebuttal.

Concerning the alleged collapse of manufacturing in the United States, it's important to recall that there's been a reduction in the number of factory jobs, but no reduction at all in what we produce. As Bruce Bartlett pointedly observes, "Contrary to the widespread perception, we're not manufacturing fewer goods than we used to; in fact, Americans are producing more goods than ever before. Manufacturing employs a smaller percentage of American workers because other sectors of the economy have grown faster, and manufacturing requires fewer workers today because of the phenomenal increase in workers' productivity." In fact, manufacturing output (in constant dollars) more than doubled between 1975 and 2009, according to the Bureau of Labor Statistics, and the United States remains by far the world's leading exporter of manufactured goods. We now create nearly $4 trillion of durable and nondurable goods every year right here in America, while importing less than half as much. The reason that fewer workers find employment in manufacturing is that each of those workers can achieve more at the plant thanks to improved technology, efficiency, and what futurist gurus of forty years ago used to call "automation." We now use fewer people to produce more goods—a positive, not a negative development for the economy. Moreover, we're not alone in the decrease in the number of factory jobs due to greater efficiency. The *Wall Street Journal* reported in 2003 that U.S. manufacturing employment declined by 11 percent in the previous seven years—a decline identical to that of the world average. China during the same period lost

LETTING TIGER WOODS PLAY GOLF

The argument for unimpeded international commerce relies on the principle of comparative advantage—that all economic entities benefit when each one manages to concentrate on what it does best. This theory, developed by British economist David Ricardo in the early nineteenth century, argues that it makes no sense for any family or any nation for that matter to attempt to produce everything: wealth and living standards will increase by purchasing goods and resources from other individuals or societies that can provide them more cheaply. The economist Paul Samuelson uses the example of a brilliant lawyer who knows he's not only the best attorney but also the best secretary in his community. He therefore might feel tempted to achieve an unnecessary self-sufficiency, interrupting his legal work to perform his own secretarial chores, but he would certainly sacrifice money in the process. It would work far better to hire a secretary at relatively low wages and to pay her to perform her less-specialized labor, allowing the lawyer to earn far more money doing the work only he could do.

According to Matthew J. Slaughter of Dartmouth,

Hard-working Americans are not going to excel at everything. Comparative advantage says each country should concentrate its time and talent on the particular goods and services it is productive at relative to the rest of the world. It should then export those items abroad and in exchange import the goods and services at which other countries are relatively more productive.

Countries cannot have a comparative advantage at everything. That's okay. Tiger Woods is better off spending his time playing golf, not painting his house. Similarly, imports from overseas do not represent failure. They raise standards of living.

15 percent of its industrial jobs, with an even more acute need than the United States to shift displaced factory workers to more modern, technologically advanced enterprises.

Regarding the huge trade deficit, Daniel Griswold of the Cato Institute makes the important point that trade surpluses or deficits tell you nothing meaningful about a nation's economic vitality or standard of living. Japan, Germany, Russia, and China all enjoy big trade surpluses, but that doesn't make them international "winners." Griswold asks, "If trade surpluses are so great, why has Japan suffered more than a decade of stagnation and why are Germans saddled with chronic double-digit unemployment? How many workers in 'loser' America would willingly swap places with their counterparts in such 'winners' as Brazil, Russia and China? No thanks."

Regarding the environment, the spread of free markets and free trade has facilitated international cooperation on global challenges, including climate changes. The nations that are most resistant to cross-border commerce display some of the worst environmental records in the world, while the International Chamber of Commerce rightly noted, "It is the countries which have embraced and promoted globalization—the industrialized democracies—that have done the most to protect the environment." Rioters at the "Battle in Seattle" promoted the idiotic notion that American companies threatened to exploit and despoil pristine paradises in remote corners of the world where the inhabitants purportedly lived in perfect harmony with nature. In fact, starving subsistence farmers and herdsman are far more likely than multinational corporations to poach endangered species in precious wildlife reserves, or to use slash-and-burn tactics to roll back the rain forest. To some extent, conservation and environmental sensitivity count as luxuries for the developed world, and by far the best way to spread those values involves the improvement in living standards made possible by globalization. In his feisty 2000 book *Fighting the Wrong Enemy: Antiglobal Activists and Multinational Enterprises,* Edward M. Graham dispenses with the treasured radical idea of reestablishing a low-impact, low-pressure, premodern existence. "A worldwide return to simple, organic, rural lifestyles is no answer at all," he writes. "Three quarters of China's population already has the lifestyle—and most of them are desperate to escape." In that process of escape, the Chinese have compiled a record on pollution that's far more destructive than those of the United States and Western Europe.

ENTREPRENEURIAL ILLUSIONS

The nostalgic yearning for simpler, sweeter, more intimate associations has become a ubiquitous response to the demands and complexities of twenty-first-century life, fueling idealized notions of small farms, small towns, and even small business. The glorification of struggling start-ups and other new and modest enterprises has become nearly as misleading as the one-dimensional demonization of big multinational corporations.

In the end, small businesses won't single-handedly save our world any more than big businesses will destroy it.

Nevertheless, the press still clings to the romantic idea that it's minor firms and not the corporate power structure that will miraculously lead the way to economic revival. "Small Businesses Vital to Economic Recovery Go Bankrupt" warned a worried headline in *USA Today,* while the story never explained why little operations (5.5 million of which employ fewer than twenty-five people) would determine the economic destiny of a nation of 300 million. Meanwhile, an approving front-page story in the *Washington Post* (July 11, 2009) described efforts by the Obama administration to divert money from the "$700 billion rescue program for the banking system and make it available to millions of small businesses, which officials say are essential to any economic recovery because they employ so many people." Later in the story, reporter David Cho strengthened his case by explaining that "some economists estimate that small businesses, defined as firms with fewer than 500 workers, employ most of the country's work force."

Actually, precise numbers from the Small Business Administration make such "estimates" unnecessary: according to the most recent figures, the national workforce is split almost precisely between firms with fewer than 500 employees (60,223,710) and those with more than 500 (59,693,425). These statistics also seem somewhat misleading, since most people might classify a business with more than 400 people as "big" or at least "medium-sized," rather than small. Unequivocally minor firms (those with fewer than twenty-five employees) engage less than 21 percent of the total workforce, while very large companies, with more than a thousand on payroll, employ fully 44 percent of all U.S. workers.

Sentimentalists may relish the notion that little, underdog enterprises with limited resources will somehow drag lumbering corporate behemoths back to prosperity, but there's no logical or empirical reason to believe that the economy has ever worked that way. In a brilliantly argued 2008 book, *The Illusions of Entrepreneurship*, economics professor Scott Shane of Case Western Reserve University provides harsh truths to balance small-business dreams. For instance, he shows that the average new venture will fail within five years of its launch, and even successful founders who have built their businesses for ten years will typically earn 35 percent less than they would have if they had continued to work for others.

"Very simply, the popular belief that we can cause economic growth to increase by upping the rate at which new firms are formed is probably incorrect," Shane writes. "Let's start with some basic facts. Very few people work in new firms. According to research by Zoltan Acs and Catherine Arrington, companies less than two years old and with at least one employee account for only 1 percent of employment in the United States."

When it comes to creating *new* jobs, start-ups play a similarly underwhelming role, with research at the University of Maryland showing that one-year-old firms created less than 7 percent of new jobs in a pattern that looks consistent "across industries, regions, firm size, and type of firm ownership." These easily available numbers didn't prevent the Committee on Small Business of the House of Representatives from fatuously announcing in a 2009 press release that "small businesses create 80 percent of all new jobs and drive innovation in virtually every field."

Concerning such groundless pronouncements, Scott Shane asks, "So what should you think about the often-made statement that entrepreneurs create half of all new jobs created in this country? . . . Clearly, if an entrepreneur is someone who created a firm that is one year old, then this statement is just plain wrong. . . . Studies conducted in the United States, Sweden, and Germany show that each cohort of new firms employs more people in its first year than it employs in any year after that. For instance, the cohort of new employer firms founded in the United States in 1998 employed 798,066 people in its first year but only 670,111 people in 2002. In other words, the number of jobs lost by new firms that close down in their second year, third year, fourth year, and so on exceeds the number of jobs added by the expansion of the new firms that survive." In short, the net result of business start-ups is to lose jobs rather than to create them.

The public prefers to ignore such realities because of the cherished American view of the small businessman as an indomitable, heroic figure whose courage and hard work have always powered the national economy. In fact, Shane writes, "The typical entrepreneur is not a special person with hidden psychological powers that allow him to build great companies or great wealth; he's a middle-aged white guy who just wants to earn a living and doesn't want to work for somebody else. The typical entrepreneur could be your next door neighbor—and he might not be your most successful neighbor. People are more likely to start businesses if they are unemployed, have changed jobs often, and have made less money in their previous employment."

"HINDERING OUR ECONOMIC WELL-BEING"

Professor Shane (whose fine book bears the unwieldy subtitle "The Costly Myths That Entrepreneurs, Investors, and Policy

Makers Live By") concludes with a plea to face the truth:. "Having more start-ups in a country or region doesn't cause more economic growth. Moreover, start-ups don't generate as many jobs as most people think, and the jobs that they create aren't as good as the jobs in existing companies. . . . Our sense that the typical new business provides a great deal of benefit for its founder, his employees and customers, and society at large is also wrong. Our myths about entrepreneurship, and the policies we have developed in response to them, are leading too many people to become entrepreneurs, causing financial hardship for many, and hindering our economic well-being."

Aside from the consistently sobering data on outcomes for new businesses, common sense dictates that smaller firms will always play a less significant role in the economy than their older, bigger brothers. An unusually successful start-up may double its payroll after just five years, going from five employees to ten and adding five new jobs. Meanwhile, the big company up the street, with a thousand employees, will expand its workforce only 5 percent and still add ten times the number of new positions—fifty—as the little guy. The stability, security, and benefits of those jobs in big business will almost certainly offer more, including a vastly greater likelihood of receiving generous health care coverage.

On another contentious contemporary issue, bigger companies will also prove far more likely to conform to social and legal norms. Americans disagree sharply over what to do about illegal immigration, but nearly all of us consider it inappropriate for business owners to shrug their shoulders or wink at the rules and hire undocumented workers at hardship salaries. A 2009 report for the Pew Research Center by Jeffrey S. Passel estimates that the national labor force includes 8.3 million unauthorized immigrants—5.4 percent of all workers, compared with 4.3 percent in 2003. These mostly low-skilled laborers are naturally concentrated in jobs classically associated with small businesses—farming (25 percent); building, groundskeeping, and maintenance (19 percent); food preparation and serving (12 percent)—for a total of 56 percent of all illegal workers. On the other hand, only a small percentage of the undocumented worked in positions most often found at large firms—production (10 percent), transportation, and material moving (7 percent). Another 17 percent toiled in construction, which can mean either a little or a big company. In any event, the numbers strongly suggest that big businesses, with their human resources departments and more bureaucratic procedures, are far less likely to hire illegal immigrants (and far more likely to be busted in immigration raids if they do). It only stands to reason that undocumented workers would cluster at smaller businesses with more informal and easygoing atmospheres and procedures.

For similar reasons, outrageous and abusive behavior may go longer undetected (or at least uncorrected) at small businesses than big firms. The Burr Oak Cemetery in Alsip, Illinois, provides an especially sickening example—with four employees of the traditionally African-American burial ground arrested in the summer of 2009 and charged with digging up some 300 bodies so they could fill existing graves with the corpses of new paying customers. On learning that the remains of their family members had been carelessly tossed into double or triple unmarked graves, tearful and horrified former patrons said they felt attracted to Burr Oaks in the first place by the down-to-earth, family-like atmosphere of a classical small business. The sheer number of employees at a large facility like, say, the celebrated Forest Lawn in Los Angeles, would have made it far less likely that the cemetery scam could continue for decades before some conscientious employee saw the criminality and blew the whistle.

And speaking of whistle-blowing, the most shameless and predatory corporate criminal in history actually used a small business rather than a big company to steal billions from his customers. Bernie Madoff once employed 200 people in the well-respected and profitable trading section of his business, but the investment division of Bernard L. Madoff Investment Securities, where he operated his $64.8 billion Ponzi scheme, employed only 24 people at its height. Other famous Wall Street scandals of course unfolded at big, established prestigious firms—like Drexel, Burnham, Lambert in the 1980s. But the sheer audacity and outrageousness of Madoff's many years of scamming his best friends and favored charities would have been much easier to inspect, detect, and reject at a larger company with more built-in checks and balances.

MORE SIGNIFICANT THAN SENSE OR CENTS

No one could suggest that Bernie Madoff and the Burr Oaks Cemetery count in any way as typical of small businesses, any more than Enron and WorldCom accurately represent the true nature of big corporations. Nevertheless, these recent outrages should help to shrink the huge gap in public perceptions and "confidence" polls that regularly rank small business at the top and big companies near the bottom. The persistent preference for firms that are newer and smaller over proven, prosperous, responsibly managed companies owes nothing to logic or history and everything to sentimentality and, in many cases, family memories.

For me, the very term *small business* conjures recollections of early childhood in Philadelphia when I used to come back from nursery school to spend every afternoon with my grandmother. After my grandfather's death (long before my birth) she teamed with her unmarried sister (my jovial Great-Aunt Irene) and bought a row house with a tiny storefront in its bottom story. There, the two elderly ladies spent nearly twenty years operating a "variety store" in which they sold an unpredictable collection of oddly assorted stuff (rubber bands, chewing gum, pencils, underwear, baseball cards, dolls, toy soldiers, and other treasures) to schoolchildren and neighbors. They would sit in the living room, watching wrestling or soap operas on their circular, wood-encased black-and-white TV while they toiled away at piecework assembling hair nets, but then rush up and into the store to wait on customers whenever the little bell jingled at the front door. Years later, it still seems unimaginable to me that they earned enough to pay bills from the meager pennies they made on selling a ball-and-jacks or a pair of socks. Nevertheless, they loved their customers, who loved them back, enjoying their German accents and courtly Old World kindliness and the convenience of the tiny shop that stayed open till odd hours.

Of course, there's also an association with my late father—starting his first high-tech "opto-electronics" company when I was still a teenager, and filling the family study with his blue pipe smoke and the sounds of Vivaldi from the record player while he struggled late at night with forms and formulas and bills and balance sheets. He loved every aspect of the process, even when debts accumulated and wiser heads told him to go back to his jobs at a defense company or a university. The Scott

Shane figures show how gifted or fortunate he was, to start two different enterprises and to survive and thrive both times, never gathering more than 100 employees but inspiring and coddling those who stayed with him. In his belted bathrobe and slippers on those long business-building nights, he taught me to savor the arrival of the dawn more than the comforts of sleep.

There is, finally, romance and adventure connected to small business and entrepreneurship, no matter how ill-advised or pedestrian these new ventures may be. Americans have always loved playing the long shot and hoping to overcome the odds in a nation that began with its own irrational series of struggling start-ups at Jamestown, Plymouth, Massachusetts Bay, New Amsterdam, and Philadelphia. The battered economy may not count on little, dicey enterprises to power the hopes for recovery and restoration, but at least these small businesses, even when run by old men and women, connect with the spirit of youth— of the all-American triumph of hope over experience. In an eternally youthful nation of new beginnings and fresh starts, that spirit provides a stronger, more durable connection than any consideration of sense—or cents.

"Government Is More Fair
and Reliable Than Business"

New York City employment bureau, opening day, 1914

$100,000 PER YARD

In a triumph of bureaucratic innovation, Seattle officials tried to encourage the public to make use of a hugely expensive new transit system by banning all parking near the stations. In so doing, they provided a perfect example of government's contemptuous, reckless, and ubiquitous disregard for the people it's supposed to serve and represent.

The residents of the city tried to make sense of the puzzling and novel policy in July 2009, after the long-delayed completion of the most expensive light rail project in U.S. history. The heralded debut of Central Link, following fourteen years of controversy, cost overruns, false starts, embarrassing federal audits, endless delays, and back-to-the-drawing-board reconsiderations, left many locals deeply and openly appalled by the authorities' bizarre attempt to prevent people from using their cars to connect with the trains. The wildly controversial project (just the first stage of a vast, altogether unaffordable transit system scheduled for construction over the next thirty years) cost $2.4 billion for a meager 14-mile line—an unprecedented public investment of $171 million per mile (or nearly $100,000 per yard). The thirteen gleaming new stations feature millions of dollars' worth of eye-catching public art but not a single parking place, except for a few coveted slots at the Tukwila station currently marking the end of the line.

What's more, the imperious executives at Sound Transit decreed strict limitations even for on-street parking anywhere within a quarter mile of the lavish new stations. Anyone who attempts to park a few blocks away from the light rail line and then to board a train to get to work downtown will face a minimum fine of $44 plus potential towing charges.

"Light rail was meant to be fed by people taking the bus, walking or biking," sniffed Rick Sheridan, spokesman for the Seattle Department of Transportation. "It was not meant to be fed by cars." He insisted that "Seattle planners" looked to light rail "with a long term eye." Garages with hundreds of parking stalls "didn't fit into the vision," Sheridan told the *Seattle Times.* The grand-opening brochure for the system, festively titled *Travel Light!,* featured the following helpful explanation under the heading "Getting to the Stations": "There is *no* parking. Our best advice is take a bus, walk or ride your bike to the station. . . . Riding your bike is a great way to get to the stations. . . . We encourage you to bring a lock and park your bicycle at the staffed bicycle corrals at each station prior to boarding."

Meanwhile, potential riders stewed over their inability to use the new system, despite a total cost for construction that amounted to more than $10,000 per city household. Jammie Hunter, a resident of south Seattle's gentrifying Columbia City neighborhood, lives "about a mile away" from the nearest station, which she considers "a little more than walking distance." She originally planned to drive to the nearby terminal, park on a neighborhood street, and then enjoy a breezy, high-tech commute to downtown. But the parking restrictions (the city declared open war on "hide-and-riders") made her plan impossible and left her clueless about getting to work, especially since the transit system cut back on existing bus service to try to force citizens to use the new light rail. "Why would you invest so much taxpayer money into public transit and take away parking?" Ms. Hunter asked the *Seattle Times.* "If they want to maximize ridership, that's not the way to do it."

Jerri White, another victim of the ill-conceived edicts of visionary planners, complained that her condition (arthritis and fibromyalgia) made it impossible for her to walk or bike the half mile to Rainier Beach station as Sound Transit suggested. As director of the popular social work agency Southeast Youth and Family Services, Ms. White, fifty-three, said she'd probably begin taking her car to work, since the new bus schedule left her old, convenient route suspended.

Apologists for the huge governmental investment (local, state, and federal) in light rail insisted that the inconvenience imposed on the likes of Ms. White mattered far less than the triumphal thrill of operating a spiffy new made-in-Japan train all the way from downtown to the Seattle-Tacoma International Airport (Sea-Tac), a route comprising the full 14 miles of the new line. By car, the trip from the airport to downtown was never a particular problem, demanding no more than half an hour even in moderately heavy traffic. The light rail system, on the other hand, will almost certainly take longer for most commuters: until its final segment is finished (with completion date optimistically projected for December 2009), the line will stop well short of the airport terminal and travelers will need to trundle onto shuttle buses for the climactic leg of their adventure. In other words, a passenger hoping to get on a plane to New York or Chicago will need to take his or her luggage from home on his bicycle (or a bus), unload and board a Central Link train, ride the train for a few miles, then gather up the bags and board yet another bus, then unload again at curbside before schlepping all the stuff up to the ticket counter to arrive in glorious discomfort.

No wonder the projections of ridership for this gold-plated new system remain distinctly modest: officials hope that within a year of the grand opening, they will welcome 26,000 passengers each day—an insignificant blip in a metropolitan area of more than three million. Before the construction of light rail, only 3 percent of all Seattle-area commuters used buses or existing trains, and the other 97 percent traveled the congested freeways in cars. At best, planners claim that the new train system will raise the percentage of mass-transit commuters to 4.5 percent—and freely acknowledge that new light rail riders will include a large proportion of passengers who merely shift over from buses, providing no real reduction in the number of cars on the road. A major study by the Washington Policy Center in 2007 suggested that Sound Transit's grand plans, featuring at least 40 miles of new track, would shift at most 0.4 percent of the cars off the highways by 2030. By that time, traffic delays in the region would more than double in any event, as population growth easily outpaced the very minor additional carrying capacity by the ambitious government program.

To adjust to these stark realities, the transit planners now regularly intone that they see the Central Link system and its already planned successors as "an alternative to congestion, not a solution to congestion." In other words, for the subsidized riders who hop aboard the shiny new trains, the system may save a few minutes a day, but for the poor slobs stuck in gridlocked traffic (who aren't willing or able to bike or walk to those gaudily decorated Central Link stations) the huge public investment does absolutely nothing.

NO USE FOR HOT LATTES OR HOT CHICKS

In this regard, the Seattle experience follows the dreary and dreadful pattern established by the twenty new light rail systems constructed across the country since 1980. Analyzing the six of those systems already operating on the West Coast, the Washington Policy Center concluded flatly, "Light rail does not reduce traffic congestion. In 2005, light rail systems on the West

Coast served only about 2 percent of the work force in their service areas. On average, these systems only remove between 0.39 percent and 1.1 percent of cars from the roadway."

Statistics from every region of the United States, in fact, show no evidence that even the most costly and elaborate new rail systems succeed in reducing traffic or trimming commute times. Every year the Texas Transportation Institute issues a "mobility report" measuring the typical travel delays, excess fuel consumption, and congestion cost for commuters in the nation's major urban areas. Amazingly, all five of the most congested and traffic-plagued cities either invested in gigantic recent mass-transit experiments designed to reduce that congestion (Los Angeles, Atlanta, Miami, Dallas–Fort Worth) or else they boasted older, well-established, vast rail systems much-praised by urban planners (New York City, Chicago). The rankings in this mobility report don't prove that mass transit causes gridlock, but they likewise give no indication that these projects do anything at all to solve the problem. Of the fifteen cities with the worst delays, every one of them has invested huge sums in rail mass transit, without visible improvement on the highways. Ironically, Seattle already enjoyed a favorable rating in terms of congestion (number fifteen on the list) even before the opening of the most-expensive-ever new light rail monstrosity.

Even after these systems go into operation, they continue to bleed money. Downtown Detroit's infamous People Mover train was completed in 1987, with officially projected daily ridership of 67,700. In the first year of operation, the system drew only 11,000 daily riders, and today the patronage has slipped even further, with only 7,500 lonely passengers, or a mere 2.5 percent of capacity. The People Mover, in other words, serves less than one-ninth of the projected passenger load, with no impact whatever on traffic (Detroit ranks as tenth-worst in the country). Meanwhile, the bankrupt city spends at least $3 to transport each of the passengers, who contribute a fare of only fifty cents. As the Washington Policy Center aptly concluded, "Light rail is expensive and it requires significant public assistance. On average, West Coast light rail systems need taxpayer subsidies to pay for 73 percent of operations and 100 percent of capital improvements each year." If these ill-conceived projects were injured horses, merciful owners would shoot them to stop the pain; if they were private businesses, they'd close down to end the limitless losses.

And speaking of losses, Seattle commuters on the Central Link system will pay between $1.75 and $2.50 per trip, while drawing a subsidy from taxpayers that may amount to *at least* $10 per trip—even if the highly dubious, wildly optimistic predictions of ridership come true. As I suggested on my radio show, Sound Transit could have lured far more passengers onto buses (without spending $171 million a mile for new track) by offering passengers free lattes on every trip. They might have even followed the internationally publicized example of some local espresso stands that drew customers with "bikini baristas" serving their hot drinks. At far lower cost than building and operating Central Link (and the other planned lines), Sound Transit could have hired lovely and skimpily clad "ride attendants" to serve the free refreshments for every downtown bus trip. Even paying top dollar to hire the most cheerful and alluring young ladies would save big money—and draw more customers—than investing literally hundreds of millions in ripping up streets, building underground stations that resemble the Bat Cave, and commissioning fanciful public art (including Victoria

Fuller's *Global Garden Shovel,* a "35 foot blue spade covered with bronze vegetables").

Unlike private businesses trying to attract new customers, government agencies like Sound Transit would never even consider offering free drinks or sexy servers, not because it's beneath their dignity (is anything really beneath the dignity of a career transit bureaucrat?) but because they don't depend on patrons to pay their bills. They will still receive their operating subsidies, no matter how empty their handsomely appointed train cars. Unlike the for-profit streetcar and commuter rail companies that once served most American cities (including Seattle), the bosses of government transit aren't in the people-pleasing business. As Detroit's glittering triumph with the modern marvel People Mover conclusively demonstrates, the public continues to fork over tax money to keep these projects going even when they draw only a tiny fraction of the projected usage. The taxpayers provide this funding not as a matter of generosity but as victims of compulsion, regularly disregarded and even reviled by arrogant officials who believe they serve the public best when they defy its wishes most flagrantly.

In Seattle, voters turned down proposed rail systems four times since 1968, but advocates kept coming back with cunningly repackaged efforts to achieve their ends; they finally succeeded (by the narrowest of margins) to win voter approval in a low-turnout election in 1996. My first ballot as a resident of Washington State after our arrival in the Northwest involved a proud, passionate "no" vote on light rail, but we're still saddled with helping to finance the fiasco. After construction finally began, even the resolutely pro-transit *Seattle Times* reported that "neighbors endured hardships, starting with power outages and runoff flooding in Rainier Valley.

Screeching train wheels disturbed residents near the Duwamish River, and this month neighbors on the west slope of Beacon Hill said huge power lines marred their views. More than $15 million in government aid went to businesses that lost customers, and some merchants folded or were ousted by land condemnations along Martin Luther King Jr. Way South." Parents groups complained bitterly about the risk to their kids caused by speeding trains at street level; Sound Transit shrugged at the problem, predicting at least thirty "serious" accidents in the course of every year. Had private enterprise attempted to impose this sort of discomfort and misery on a skeptical public, lawsuits and complaints to government agencies might have stopped or at least altered the grand plans. As it happened, however, legal and regulatory authorities proved reluctant to interfere with their fellow "public servants"; in this rigged game, the refs and one of the competing teams wore the same uniforms onto the field.

Considering the nation's recent experience with mass transit and other bureaucratic initiatives, it defies both experience and common sense that so many Americans maintain their touchingly naïve faith that the pure-souled and disinterested idealists in government will serve people more reliably than the greedy go-getters of the private sector. This widespread, childlike belief that unselfish public efforts invariably trump profit-seeking schemes in the free market gives traction to Obama administration efforts to swell the federal role in health care, as well as other initiatives at "reform." One of the most pervasive and persistent big lies about American business maintains that government planners out to make history always perform more responsively and responsibly than competitive firms out to make a buck.

CORRUPTION AND CUPIDITY, DISAPPOINTMENT AND DESPAIR

The true believers who cling most passionately to their trust in collective, taxpayer-funded endeavors never seem to confront the obvious challenge to their confidence: the complete, consistent lack of real-world evidence that political leadership works more effectively, or even more compassionately, than the institutions of the private sector. For generations, examples of bureaucratic inefficiency and incompetence have simultaneously amused and appalled the American people. The corruption and cupidity of the political class make headlines at the federal, state, and local level. In every field of endeavor, government operations produce more than their share of disappointment and even despair, especially when they compete directly with private options.

Consider the most obvious and salient recent examples:

- The United States Postal Service struggles for survival while private delivery services manage to adjust to the troubled economy and enjoy booming business. Most recently, the Postal Service faced yearly losses of more than $7 billion and planned painful elimination of some 3,000 local offices and perhaps 10,000 jobs. Rapid, regular increases in postage charges haven't helped, nor has the emergence of the faster, cheaper, more reliable alternative of e-mail. Nevertheless, Federal Express and United Parcel Service continue to serve eager customers and draw massive revenues. In 2008, the two delivery companies combined for $89.4

billion in business, compared with $74.9 billion for the taxpayer-supported, sclerotic USPS.

- By the same token, private schools outperform public schools almost everywhere, producing better results from their students at much lower cost—usually less than half, according to University of Maryland economist John Lott. Even in the grittiest inner-city neighborhoods, Catholic schools (throwing open their doors to non-Catholics) register notably better test scores than the public alternatives, even when they draw student bodies of largely similar ethnic and socioeconomic backgrounds. Writing in the *Washington Post* (April 6, 2008), Andrew Coulson calculated the real cost per student in the floundering District of Columbia public schools as a breathtaking $25,000 per year, while noting that "total per pupil spending at D.C.-area private schools—among the most upscale in the nation—averages about $10,000 less." Across the country, annual spending per student in K–12 public schools more than doubled between 1970 and 2005, from $4,060 to $9,266 (in constant 2007 dollars), while reading scores at all levels remained stubbornly flat. Public school budgetary problems stemmed in large measure from the addition of new armies of bureaucrats and administrators who contributed nothing to the classroom; a review in 2000 by Claremont Colleges discovered that government schools spend 40 percent of their money on nonteacher costs, compared with less than 20 percent for private institutions. Meanwhile, federal education funding soared (increasing 138 percent per student since 1985) with no discernible benefit—except for the 5,000 employees at the famously feckless federal Department of Education, with its bizarrely bloated budget of $68.6 billion.

- In health care, the most ambitious government initiatives produced similar results, with much higher costs and no superior outcomes. In July 2009, Jeffrey Anderson completed a forty-year study for the Pacific Research Institute concluding that "since 1970, Medicare and Medicaid's cost have risen one-third more, per patient, than the combined costs of all other health care in America—the vast majority of which is purchased privately. . . . Medicare and Medicaid used to cost $20 less per patient than other care. Now they cost $1,836 more. (And that's even without the Medicare prescription-drug benefit.) In fact, if the costs of Medicare and Medicaid had risen only as much as the costs of all other health care in America, then . . . that savings of $201 billion would have amounted to more than $1,750 per American household last year alone." The finest hospital facilities and research centers remain private and independent—like the Cleveland Clinic, the Fred Hutchinson Center in Seattle, and the Mayo Clinic in Minnesota, which took a courageous stand in the midst of the bitter health care debate in the summer of 2009 against further government intrusion into our medical system.

- Amtrak, the nationalized rail passenger system (with all its preferred stock now owned by the lucky federal government), remains a singularly stunning example of bureaucratic ineptitude and wastefulness. As Edward L. Hudgins reported in a paper for the Cato

Institute (October 8, 2003), "Each year since its creation as a passenger railroad owned and operated by the federal government, Amtrak has promised it would break even, with its revenues covering its costs. It never has. Instead the American taxpayers have had to waste at least $25 billion to cover all its deficits. And what has the public received for its money? . . . Amtrak accounted for only three tenths of 1 percent of all trips taken in 2000; twice as many people took trips by small private planes. It's political pressure that keeps money-losing, half-empty trains running 12-hour routes when for not much more money, one could fly between the cities served by those trains in an hour." Actually, Hudgins understates the epochal inefficiency. My friend Stephen Moore, senior economics writer for the *Wall Street Journal* editorial page, reports that "the average taxpayer subsidy per Amtrak rider is $100 or 40 percent of the total per-passenger cost. Even this figure doesn't adequately express how hugely inefficient some long-distance routes are today. For example, the average subsidy to a New York–Los Angeles rider exceeds $1,000. The estimated round trip subsidy per passenger for a Denver–Chicago trip is $650." In other words, for the cost of the subsidy alone the government could not only buy an airline ticket, but in most cases even provide a first-class ticket. Moore concludes that "it's a myth that Amtrak simply could not survive under private ownership and operation. There is no law of nature or economics that says that trains must lose money. Because of government control, however, Amtrak costs are far higher than necessary. Amtrak provides especially unprofitable services for political reasons, and it is hamstrung by archaic work rule provisions that make it more expensive than other travel options. For example, federal law requires Amtrak to pay up to six years of severance pay to workers who are laid off." Like other critics of the system, he suggests that the public could benefit by privatization of selected routes, with numerous capable companies expressing interest in the heavily used Northeast Corridor service. In the United Kingdom, a similar takeover by Virgin brought ridership to levels unseen since the 1950s.

- The redundancy in staffing for a lumbering behemoth like Amtrak pales in comparison with the duplicative essence of the federal bureaucracy itself. Not even the most seasoned Washington insider could explain or even recognize the literally thousands of agencies, programs, and departments that regularly overlap in their express purposes. At tax time in 2005, the Heritage Foundation made a detailed tally of some of the most grotesquely redundant sets of federal operations, some of them coexisting in neighboring corners of the bureaucracy, including

  342 economic development programs

  130 programs serving the disabled

  130 programs serving at-risk youth

  90 early-childhood development programs

  50 homeless assistance programs

  27 teen pregnancy programs

  19 programs fighting substance abuse

If these semi-independent initiatives are all function-
ing as they should, could we make even more dramatic
progress with fifty more teen pregnancy programs?

- Yearly revelations of flagrant callousness and waste in
every federal department give the lie to claims of a
dedicated and attentive federal bureaucracy, proudly
committed to selfless public service. In July 2009, former Oklahoma congressman Ernest Istook reported
for the Heritage Foundation that "the backlog of Social Security disability claims rose to 750,000 individuals in recent years, with average waits of about a year
and a half to get an appeals hearing. Each applicant
had to be disabled a full year before they could even
apply—and then wait on the bureaucracy for many
months more. Each year, 22 million Americans receive IRS checks of up to $4,700, collectively $44 billion. Almost one third of the claims are fraudulent,
according to the IRS that sends out the checks. . . . Ten
thousand or more dead people also received 'stimulus'
checks from Social Security. Many had been dead for
years." Unfortunately, the Social Security Administration provided no confirmation on the effectiveness of
this stimulus spending on the deceased.

- In yet another miracle of imaginative investment, the
Department of Defense found an even more wasteful
way to spend money on transportation than Amtrak or
Seattle's light rail. In 2005, an audit revealed that over
the course of six years (1997–2003) the Pentagon purchased then left unused some 270,000 commercial airline tickets *at a total cost of $100 million.* Amazingly
enough, the DOD never even bothered to get a refund

for these fully refundable, full-price tickets. Meanwhile, over at the Department of Agriculture (an anachronistic monstrosity with a $95 billion annual budget and 105,778 indispensable employees), another audit showed that busy workers had diverted millions in personal purchases through their government-issued credit cards. As Brian Riedl reported in a Heritage Foundation "Backgrounder" (April 4, 2005), "Sampling 300 employees' purchases over six months, investigators estimated that 15 percent abused their government credit cards at a cost of $5.8 million. Taxpayer-funded purchases included Ozzy Osbourne concert tickets, tattoos, lingerie, bartender school tuition, car payments and cash advances."

- Even the National Park Service, the public's sentimental favorite among federal programs, has degenerated into the sort of haphazard and arrogant operation that would never survive in the private sector. As a boy, I gleefully visited dozens of national parks with my camping-mad parents, checking off each visit from a master list of the natural treasures and yearning to reach them all. We always felt thrilled and inspired to drive past the big wooden welcome signs with their distinctive arrowhead NPS logo. As we entered protected federal territory, the landscape instantly looked more spectacular and the air itself tasted sweeter. I loved the rangers with their gray-green uniforms and Smokey the Bear hats, the visitor center displays of stuffed animals and three-dimensional topographical maps, the campfire lectures every evening, and the sense of exhilarating fellowship in the woods. Nevertheless, all recent reports document trouble in paradise. The most popular parks now suffer from overcrowding, air pollution, and other out-of-place urban ills, while subpar maintenance and pinched budgets leave beloved and sometimes historic facilities looking shabby and run-down. In May 2007, the *Christian Science Monitor* reported that the "backlog in park maintenance and resource protection—upkeep for some 8,000 miles of roads, 1,500 bridges, 400 dams, and 30,000 structures, plus protecting meadows, streams and other wildlife habitat from the wear and tear of hiking boots—totals between $4.5 billion and $9.7 billion. At Yosemite, that backlog tops $100 million, including the removal of crumbling asphalt from trails, a new wastewater plant, and the replacement of camping areas washed away by a 1997 flood." Meanwhile, with increasingly strained staff resources, lawless activity—including gang violence and the cultivation of illegal drugs—increasingly afflicts Park Service lands. Not surprisingly, the public has responded to these challenges with reduced attendance. Astonishingly, total visits to the park system peaked in 1987. Since that time, the nation's population has increased *by more than 50 million* and the government (with much fanfare) dedicated ten new national parks, but the public's visits to those natural wonderlands actually declined. *USA Today* reported in 2009 that the leadership of the Park Service committed itself to a bold new effort to "stir interest" on the part of an indifferent public in its 391 properties, spending $754 million in federal stimulus funds to "spruce up deteriorating facilities and trails at places such as the Grand Canyon." According to

NPS spokesman David Barna, "Parks haven't been in great shape in the last few years."

In 2009, increasingly worried administrators tried a promotional experiment: waiving entrance fees (generally $25 at the most popular parks) on three busy summer weekends. President Obama and his family also paid brief, well-publicized visits to Yellowstone and Grand Canyon to help spark interest in the struggling system, and the public responded with a notable uptick in attendance, finally recognizing that "national parks are economical destinations," according to spokeswoman Kathy Kupper. As a thought experiment, imagine that a private corporation (rather than a stuffy bureaucracy) had been running the vast system of recreation areas and nature preserves. Is it conceivable that a for-profit enterprise would have blithely allowed its national brand to decay for decades, while its priceless properties remained underutilized and poorly maintained, drawing a steadily smaller share of the vastly expanded market? To provide an easy answer to that question, consider the record of the Disney theme parks—noted for their sparkling maintenance, immaculate grooming (with litter collected many times each day), aggressive marketing, and ingenious knack for bonding with an eager public. No one would suggest seriously that Disney "imagineers" should take over the administration of Yellowstone (would the bears wear mouse ears?), or that national park admission fees should rise to Disneyland levels (now more than $70 for adults). But there's no reason that America's natural wonders (with facilities subsidized by more than $2 billion in annual taxpayer dollars) should receive less respectful treatment from their administrators than the synthetic wonders of the Magic Kingdom receive from theirs, or that Mount Rainier National Park should prove less attentive (and attractive) to its hordes of visitors than, say, Disney's masterfully presented Animal Kingdom attraction in Orlando.

LOGIC, NOT MAGIC

The consistent contrast between private-sector energy and governmental ineptitude turns up not only in a domestic context but also in international comparisons of growth. Since 1994, the *Wall Street Journal* and the Heritage Foundation have collaborated in compiling an annual Index of Economic Freedom, ranking the nations of the world based on the extent that they rely on free markets rather than centralized command-and-control economies. Year after year, the governments that enforce the lowest tax rates and impose the least intrusive and onerous regulations deliver the most robust growth rates for their people. In 2009, Terry Miller (coeditor of the index with Kim R. Holmes) reported, "The positive correlation between economic freedom and national income is confirmed yet again by this year's data. The freest countries enjoy per capita incomes over 10 times higher than those in countries ranked as 'repressed.'" Most recently, the United States ranked sixth of the 179 nations on the list—behind Hong Kong, Singapore, Australia, Ireland, and New Zealand (in that order). No one can maintain that the surging economies of the top five result from happy accident or favorable historical circumstance; as recently as a generation ago, Ireland counted as one of the least developed (and most war-torn) nations of Europe, and Singapore (along with other Asian "Tigers") had only begun to emerge from colonialism and World War II occupation. At the same time, the nations at the very bottom of the list (Burma, Cuba, Zimbabwe, and North Korea) all suffered from wretched political and economic leadership, and once enjoyed far higher living standards and brighter prospects than they do today.

The glaring disparities between North Korea (the most blighted nation on earth, according to the index) and its neighbor South Korea (ranked fortieth this year) offer an especially dramatic comparison between a society in which the government controls every aspect of economic life and one with a boisterously competitive business system. Despite virtually identical ethnicity, cultural background, and distribution of natural resources, South Korea tops North Korea in per capita gross domestic product by an almost unimaginable ratio of twelve-to-one. Guy Sorman, veteran professor at the Paris Institute of Political Sciences, makes similar observations about the practical impact of free markets in his fascinating and hugely persuasive 2009 book *Economics Does Not Lie.* He notes that "good economic policies" resulted in "the reconstruction of Western Europe after World War II in less than thirty years, followed by that of Eastern Europe beginning in 1990. Over the two last decades until the 2008 crisis, good economics lifted 800 million people out of mass poverty, particularly in India and China. In civilizations once thought to be stagnant—Japan, Korea, Turkey—good economic strategies have engendered prosperity." By contrast, "the collectivization of land—in Russia during the thirties, in China during the fifties, in Tanzania during the

ARCTIC EXPLORERS
DISCOVER CAPITALIST ADVANTAGES

Professor Jonathan Karpoff of the University of Washington devised an ingenious means for exposing and comprehending governmental inefficiency. His 2001 article for the *Journal of Political Economy* examined explorations of the Arctic and the North Pole from 1818 to 1909, comparing thirty-five government-sponsored expeditions with fifty-seven privately funded voyages. The government missions benefited from better funding, bigger ships, and much larger crews, but they were far more likely to end in tragedy. Six crewmen died on the average government expedition, compared with fewer than one on the privately funded trips, while the chances of losing a ship were twice as high among the government voyages. Despite the greater sacrifice, higher funding levels, and larger crews, the governmental explorers achieved only one of the six major Arctic discoveries; the less lavishly funded and much smaller private crews accomplished the other five.

The results reflected some of the inevitable advantages of private-sector, for-profit undertakings over official, bureaucratic projects. The private Arctic expeditions were less wasteful, and readjusted their strategies far more quickly and readily in response to past mistakes. The governmental voyagers found themselves hampered by the need to navigate bureaucratic channels, which were even more dangerous than icebergs; leadership by committee and political factors undermined both planning and execution. Most significantly, the private journeys responded more directly and immediately to maximize success. The sponsors and decision-makers back home risked their own funds, and stood to benefit directly from the ventures—leading to better, more agile decisions than those made by planners who spent taxpayer money. As Milton Friedman unforgettably pointed out, "Nobody spends somebody else's money as carefully as he spends his own."

sixties—starved hundreds of millions of peasants. . . . The nationalization of enterprises and the expulsion of entrepreneurs ruined Argentina during the forties and Egypt during the fifties. India's licensing regime froze the country's development from 1949 to 1991."

The negative impact of centrally planned, overtaxed, and heavily regulated economic decisions proved altogether predictable, just as the surging productivity and rising living standards associated with free enterprise flowed from logic, not magic. In his 1962 classic *Man, Economy, and State,* the late Austrian School economist Murray Rothbard wrote, "The well-known inefficiencies of government operation are not empirical accidents, resulting perhaps from the lack of a civil service tradition. They are *inherent* in all government enterprise. . . . There is no way that government, even if it wanted to, could allocate its services to the most important uses and to the most eager buyers. All buyers, all uses, are artificially kept on the same plane. As a result, the most important uses will be slighted, and the government is faced with insuperable allocation problems, which it cannot solve *even to its own satisfaction*" (italics in the original).

Since an economy reflects the separate decision-making by

literally millions of its participants, decentralized power reliably promotes better decisions. No central planner, no matter how enlightened or well-intentioned, can make crucial economic decisions for masses of people better than those individuals themselves. Howard Baetjer, who teaches economics at Maryland's Towson University, succinctly explains, "Governments can spend only what they tax, or borrow away from the public; and politicians and bureaucrats don't know how to spend or invest other people's money as well as do the people themselves." Or, in the words of Richard Wagner, professor of economics at George Mason University (echoing the great Milton Friedman), "Private spending is generally more efficient than the government spending that would replace it because people act more carefully when they spend their own money than when they spend other people's money."

In his marvelous book *Freedomnomics* (2007), John Lott of the University of Maryland offers the clearest explanation I've ever encountered of the basis for governmental inefficiency. Professor Lott focuses on the distorting impact of the highly progressive U.S. tax system. According to recent figures, the top 5 percent of income earners pay 57 percent of all federal income taxes, while the bottom 50 percent pay just 3.3 percent. This means, as Lott pointedly notes, that "those who provide little of the government's income have more of a say—in the form of their combined votes—over how to spend government funds than those who provide most of the money." In other words, when voters endorse various projects and programs they are, in effect, spending someone else's money.

Lott concludes that "government spending is inherently inefficient because those who actually pay for most government services are not the ones who determine how the money is spent. . . . In private markets, you can't get people to pay more for a product than they value it. If the asking price is too high, they simply say 'no.' But there is no similar limitation on the government, which pays for things by levying taxes. And taxes are coercive—you can't refuse to pay taxes just because the government is paying more for something than you value it."

FAIRNESS OVER EFFICIENCY

Logical argument and empirical evidence lead inevitably to identical conclusions regarding economic efficiency: free-market decisions in a competitive business system lead to better results than top-down governmental directives, no matter how well-intentioned. Despite all their grandly designed "Five-Year Plans" and "New Economic Policies," socialist governments could never keep up with the headlong rush to prosperity by millions of individual decision-makers pursuing their own self-interest in free-enterprise economies. On November 18, 1956, Soviet dictator Nikita Khrushchev addressed shocked Western ambassadors at the Polish embassy and boasted of Russia's coming victory in the worldwide economic competition: "Whether you like it or not, history is on our side," he growled. "We will bury you!" In fact, Khrushchev (and his predecessors and successors) buried plenty of their fellow countrymen, but capitalism triumphed easily with its vastly superior ability to create wealth.

Sophisticated leftists no longer deny the facts of the historical record, but they deride their significance by dismissing the market's achievements as "*mere* wealth." They may concede that business functions more efficiently than government, but they simultaneously trumpet their own concerns with values far higher than efficiency. In on-air argument with the Reverend Jim Wallis, the proudly progressive founder of *Sojourners Magazine* and author of the bestselling book *God's Politics,* he's countered my praise of capitalist productivity by citing one of his favorite verses (8:36) from the Gospel According to Mark: "For what shall it profit a man, if he shall gain the whole world, and lose his own soul?"

To ardent liberals like Wallis, the essence of soulfulness is fairness, not efficiency. Government works better than the market because even if it generates fewer riches it distributes them equitably. If we all count as children of God, equally valued on the scales of eternity, then how can we justify limitless discrepancies in the way society feeds, shelters, educates, heals, and rewards its various members?

In an insightful column of April 5, 2009, Charles Krauthammer analyzed the sweeping mission of a new president. "Obama is a leveler," he wrote. "He has come to narrow the divide between rich and poor. For him the ultimate social value is fairness. Imposing it upon the American social order is his mission.

"Fairness through leveling is the essence of Obamaism. (Asked by Charlie Gibson during a campaign debate about his support for raising capital gains taxes—even if they cause a net revenue loss to the government—Obama stuck to the tax hike 'for purposes of fairness.') . . . His goal is to rewrite the American social compact, to recast the relationship between government and citizen. He wants government to narrow the nation's income and anxiety gaps. Soak the rich for reasons of revenue and justice. Nationalize health care and federalize education to grant all citizens of all classes the freedom from anxiety about health and college that the rich enjoy."

To conservatives and libertarians, of course, there's nothing fair about distributing economic rewards to people who never earned them, and it's fundamentally unjust to seize wealth from those who created it in the first place. As even the progressive hero Andrew Jackson declared in his celebrated 1832 veto of the new charter of the Bank of the United States (previously cited under Big Lie #4), "Distinctions in society will always exist under every just government. Equality of talents, of education, or of wealth can not be produced by human institutions." If those differences and divisions turn up as an eternal feature of every culture, then attempts to erase them through the application of governmental force become as arbitrary and unfair as efforts to accentuate those distinctions through favoritism for the rich. Assigning the world's goodies through the political process isn't inherently more compassionate or sensible than distributing them through the market; it's just another questionable alternative for apportioning limited resources.

Rabbi Daniel Lapin proposes an imaginative means for evaluating those various strategies, trying to devise the most sensible scheme for handing out prizes that everyone would covet. Imagine beachfront property in a hot climate, where each citizen naturally desires one of the few available lots to enjoy life by the seashore. The most obvious way to distribute those precious parcels would be through lottery, distributing the scarce land in a thoroughly indiscriminate fashion. No one could fault the objectivity of the final choice, since it's guided purely by chance, but such a decision also means that the lots might go to people who couldn't develop them as effectively, or value them as much, as their neighbors. The process will seem fair (since it's random) but the outcome is highly unlikely to provide for the most efficient use of available resources.

Another possibility would require the evaluation of the thousands of applicants to select the most deserving and suitable. This approach necessitates a committee process, or an executive judgment—in any event, a bureaucratic, quasi-governmental, inevitably subjective decision. Even with the most honorable figures in charge of the selection, the possibilities for bias and folly loom large. How many judges or land-commission members could remain utterly impartial if their close relatives applied? And anyone who's ever participated in a board meeting of any kind can readily imagine the agony of reaching agreement on the proper standard of how to determine who deserves the land most. With this approach, the process may seem suspect and unfair and the outcome may or may not bring the efficient result intended.

Finally, there's the free-market alternative—selling the scarce lots to the top bidder, and thereby determining who's willing to sacrifice the most and work the hardest to acquire the choice property. This strategy allows for an objective standard (measured numerically) in going through the process and simultaneously improves the odds for efficient development of the scarce land. Anyone who pays top dollar isn't likely to ignore the parcel, or to put up an unsightly shack by the seashore. Because of the depth of his commitment and desire, the probability increases for a beautiful mansion that can become a landmark for the whole community, or for the development of a public beach club to help earn back some of the investment that was required for the purchase. Making the highest offer for a piece of land doesn't indicate the best character necessarily, but it does express the depth of desire and commitment.

Allowing free-will agreements to trade work and goods for money (which represents someone else's work and goods) not only encourages efficient outcomes but also provides for fairness and openness in the process.

LESSONS FROM MICHAEL JACKSON

The advantages of that system became painfully clear through a boneheaded counterexample surrounding one of the more bizarre mass-media events of recent years.

The death of "King of Pop" Michael Jackson in June 2009 set off a mad scramble for limited tickets to his televised memorial service at the Staples Center in Los Angeles. With rumors of participation by entertainment legends like Stevie Wonder, Queen Latifah, Smokey Robinson, Mariah Carey, Brooke Shields, Rev. Al Sharpton, and Congresswoman Sheila Jackson Lee, the Jackson family and other organizers of the event knew they couldn't possibly accommodate all the masses of humanity who wished to attend. As a result, they sponsored a free lottery on the Internet with more than 1.8 million contestants vying for just 8,750 tickets. (Each winner would receive a pair of tickets so he or she could bring a date to the glamorous memorial.) The stupidity of this arrangement became apparent when the embarrassingly broke City of Los Angeles simultaneously began begging for donations to help defray the costs of providing police services to supervise and protect the festive mourners. A wheedling website initially pleaded for $4 million, before the disappointing crowds brought down the estimated cost and the predictably pathetic response (only $17,000 donated by fans and the bereaved) led the city to take down the humiliating bid for Internet alms and to take the necessary funds from some other important civic purpose.

In any event, the altogether obvious solution for this chaotic conundrum involved auctioning the hot seats to the memorial service rather than giving them out at random. A top-bidder distribution would at least have ensured that the people who got the tickets truly valued and desired them, while simultaneously guaranteeing a nice haul of cash to defray expenses. Apparently the Jackson family shot down any such scheme as unseemly and undignified, much preferring the solemn grandeur of an Internet lottery to select one out of a hundred lucky mourners on an utterly arbitrary basis. The same kind of decision-making prowess has no doubt contributed to the strange journey of the Pop Star's mortal remains (in their polished gold casket), with no belowground resting place even a month after his untimely demise.

Meanwhile, not even the indignant efforts of MJ's friends and family could stop the secondary scalping market that sprang up on the Internet as soon as tickets went out to the favored few. Could anyone blame a Jackson devotee for trying to pass along his randomly gotten gains for as much as $10,000 a pop?

The dark-comedy experience surrounding this tragic corpse highlighted valuable lessons on the importance of free commercial exchanges. The decision to distribute on an arbitrary basis meant that hundreds of the precious passes went unused on the day of the memorial, accounting for visible banks of empty seats. Selling those tickets on the open market might not guarantee that they went to the poorest or the most humble or the most richly deserving, but the process certainly would have ensured that the privilege went to people who valued it highly—and would have shown up on the day of the service. Even a specially chartered government commission, evaluating every applicant and drawing on the expertise and wisdom of psychologists, philosophers, theologians, and hip-hop agents, wouldn't have been able to come up with a better or more effective solution—or one less likely to provoke resentment and complaints over basic fairness.

CONTROL BY MONEY OR CONTROL BY GUNS

The governmental approach to distributing wealth relies on authority and force, while the free-market mechanism emphasizes choice. In his memorable Cato Institute speech of May 1997, the irrepressible P.J. O'Rourke echoes Ayn Rand in *Atlas Shrugged* by explaining, "If we don't want the world's wealth to be controlled by people with money, then the alternative is to have the world's wealth controlled by people with guns. And governments have guns. They have quite a few guns. Now, in theory, it is fine that the government has guns and that the guns control money because, in theory, the mugger puts his pistol down and picks up a ballot and he steals from multinational corporations instead of from you. But the reality is obviously quite different. The track record of collectivist societies in the 20th century speaks entirely for itself. Thirty million dead from closing the wealth gap in Chinese agriculture; 6 million dead from closing the commerce gap in the Ukraine; and the deaths go on and on. . . . The point is that the real alternative to the power of the rich is not power of the poor. It's just plain power."

The advantages of the market, in other words, involve far more than efficiency. They also maximize choice—or freedom.

Government, on the other hand, inevitably relies upon compulsion. You may be one of those rare, unselfish souls who proudly relish the privilege of paying taxes, but for the rest of us the prospect of prosecution and imprisonment (as illustrated by the baleful example of Wesley Snipes) plays a powerful role in encouraging cooperation. With its various dictates, the government doesn't have to cajole or seduce or persuade; it only needs to issue orders.

A silly 1990s dispute in Lebanon, Ohio, involving a local government's attempt to take over all cable TV services to make money for the town, gave rise to a clear, crisp analysis by Marc Kilmer, writing for a regional think tank called the Buckeye Institute for Public Policy Solutions (April 17, 2006). "Governments, by design, accomplish their goals by forcing people to do things. Businesses, on the other hand, must obtain the voluntary cooperation of customers by providing attractive goods and services. It's questionable whether government should even be providing services, such as cable, phone, and Internet, which private companies can provide. It's even more dubious to say that a government should be able to use its unique legal power to give itself a competitive advantage. This use of official power leads to results that only benefit the government, not the consumers."

The sort of bullying described (and properly decried) by Kilmer constitutes a far more realistic consequence of governmental power in the United States than the gulags and killing fields invoked by P.J. O'Rourke. From the site of original killing fields, a recent story in the *New York Times* illustrated that a regime can grossly abuse its power without resorting to genocide. "Cambodia's courts have been busy in recent weeks with cases of defamation, disinformation and incitement brought by the government in what critics say is part of a broad assault on civil liberties," reported the journal of record (July 21, 2009). "In the most prominent cases, two opposition politicians have been stripped of their parliamentary immunity and sued for libel" by the prime minister, Hun Sen, and his associates. The paper also reported that "Cambodian police evicted 70 families on Friday, giving them a small payment for their homes, which were on valuable land." With government inexorably increasing its authority over the private economy, is it altogether unthinkable that such abuses could occur in well-established Western democracies? Consider the well-publicized recent abuses of the "eminent domain" process, with private land seized to accomplish some "higher" public purpose.

In most of its endeavors, government constitutes an obvious monopoly—the only show in town—and a monopoly that's notoriously intolerant of competition. Like all monopolies, it operates through power rather than persuasion, coercion rather than consent; unlike private-sector monopolies and trusts, it can use the force of legislation, courts, and police to work its will.

Murray Rothbard (*Man, Economy, and State*) outlines one of the essential differences in the operations of bureaucracies and businesses: "Private firms can get funds only from consumers and investors; they can get funds, in other words, only from people who value and buy their services and from investors who are willing to risk investment of their saved funds in anticipation of profit. . . . Government, on the other hand, can get as much money as it likes. . . . Private enterprise can get funds only from satisfied, valuing customers and from investors guided by profits and losses. Government can get funds literally at its own whim."

"HERE TO HELP YOU"

Why do so many fans of big government feel unconcerned by its proprietary power and worry instead about the influence of private corporations that you can patronize or ignore according to your choice?

The core problem involves the dangerous tendency to judge intentions rather than results, and to cut government officials every sort of slack because they cloak their activities in the language of selflessness. Those who prefer publicly funded endeavors to private-sector solutions feel more instinctive trust for a government official who says "I want to help you" than they do for the honest businessman who admits "I'm hoping to help myself." They've forgotten the timeless wisdom in the marvelous statement of Henry David Thoreau: "If I know for a certainty that a man was coming to my house with the conscious design of doing me good, I should run for my life."

Ronald Reagan used to echo that statement with his frequent refrain that the most dangerous ten words in the English language were, "I'm from the government and I'm here to help you." Unfortunately, many Americans today feel reassured by such words, no matter how futile and even counterproductive the proffered help may turn out to be.

We live in an era when the president of the United States and his multitudinous acolytes applaud the ideals of "service" and "volunteerism," with slim consideration of the principles being served or the work accomplished by the volunteers. In fact, the famous "volunteers" of Bill Clinton's AmeriCorps (who now number 70,000 new recruits every year) received such generous grants and living expenses that a 1998 investigation by Citizens

Against Government Waste concluded that the agency's operational cost amounted to $27,000 per volunteer per year. Yes, these mostly youthful enthusiasts seem sincerely convinced of the rectitude of their mission (whatever it happens to be) and they all take a solemn "AmeriCorps Pledge" that seems to echo the Brown Shirts as much as the Boy Scouts:

> *I will get things done for America—to make our people*
>   *safer, smarter and healthier.*
> *I will bring Americans together to strengthen our*
>   *communities.*
> *Faced with apathy, I will take action. . . .*
> *I am an AmeriCorps member, and I will get things done*

Do these brave words make up for the fact that some of these well-paid volunteers worked in years past with organizations like the Association of Community Organizations for Reform Now (ACORN) and other borderline corrupt and nakedly political groups?

Positive motivations and gauzy sentiments should never distract from an honest evaluation of the idiotic excesses and unintentionally (but undeniably) damaging impact of some of the most ambitious government programs.

I learned poignant lessons about the dangerous nature of good intentions during our family's last years in Santa Monica, California, in the early 1990s. At almost exactly the same time, two new tenants occupied vacant storefronts in our neighborhood. One of them, a religious-based, food-for-the-homeless program, drew committed idealists with unmistakable compassion for their troubled client population. The other "grand opening" brought an artsy little coffee shop specializing in overpriced,

"NEVER TALK TO THEM OF OUR NECESSITIES BUT OF THEIR ADVANTAGES"

In his 1776 book *The Wealth of Nations*, the Scottish philosopher Adam Smith memorably framed the argument that the pursuit of self-interest most powerfully promoted human cooperation and economic advancement—not obligation, guilt, or governmental command. In perhaps the most frequently quoted passage of his hugely influential work, he concisely stated, "It is not from the benevolence of the butcher, the brewer, or the baker that we expect our dinner, but from their regard to their own self-interest. We address ourselves, not to their humanity but to their self-love, and never talk to them of our necessities but of their advantages."

frothy drinks and some fresh-baked pastries. The proprietor of that establishment worked behind the counter day and night, and if he had any other purpose in mind beyond feeding his family, he left it a well-kept secret.

Within a few months, however, it became obvious that the generous and kindly program to feed the homeless (providing free breakfast and lunch every day) that aimed to help our neighborhood actually harmed the entire area. The vagrants and wanderers, drunks, dope fiends, and psychotics began lining up before each feeding time, with the line of troubled humanity snaking through several blocks. Each day, the kindness of the religious agency brought more and more troubled souls to our beachside corner of the Los Angeles basin, inflating the local homeless population to the point of unsustainability. Ultimately, even children in the neighborhood began to notice the beer bottles, discarded syringes, litter, used condoms, human waste, shopping carts, and sleeping drunks on the sidewalks surrounding the generous do-gooders at the new service center.

Meanwhile, I began visiting the new coffee shop, appreciating the fact that the owner got up every morning before five so that early risers (like me) could enjoy a cup of steaming, delicious, fragrant java before the sun came up to light the Pacific sands. I gladly paid a few dollars to enjoy a service that notably improved my quality of daily life, providing Hemingway's "clean, well-lighted place" along with caffeinated refreshment in the somewhat lonely hours of the early morning.

In other words, it became obvious that the homeless-feeders helped to wreck the neighborhood with their selfless good intentions, while the coffee guy improved the whole area with his vigorous, effective pursuit of profit. Hopes and motives didn't matter—practical impact did.

In fact, my experience highlighted the fact that the profit motive works far more reliably than any sense of service or sacrifice to encourage beneficent behavior. The coffee shop entrepreneur would have failed and quickly closed his business had he annoyed or ignored his potential customers. He succeeded only because he made us all feel welcome and important while he toiled tirelessly to give us everything we wanted.

GOLD AND THE GOLDEN RULE

If the Golden Rule represents the essence of Western morality, then business enterprises serve as the most powerful moralizing force in our society. The only path to success involves providing other people with goods or services they need or want—doing unto these others as you would have them do unto you. The discipline of the marketplace generally rewards virtue (hard work, loyalty, reliability, consideration, kindness, cleanliness, integrity) while generally punishing vice (sloth, anger, irresponsibility). With free-enterprise transactions, you advance your own interests most formidably by serving others (sometimes literally) most effectively. There's nothing sacrilegious about turning the Golden Rule into gold, or deriving profits from the study of Prophets.

In a remarkable lecture for the Heritage Foundation in September 1998, magazine publisher (and two-time presidential contender) Steve Forbes made the case that "democratic capitalism" promotes compassion rather than arrogance, and goodness rather than greed. "To succeed in business, you have to be attentive to the needs and wants of other people," he declared. "How else do you sell them what you are offering? You have to persuade them that it is worthwhile to pay for what you're offering. Regardless of your personality, even if you have a personality that makes babies cry, you don't succeed in business unless you're attentive to the needs of your customers.

"So the remarkable thing is that commerce, free enterprise, democratic capitalism does appeal to the better angels of our nature. It encourages ambitious individuals to engage in peaceful pursuits instead of plundering their neighbors. An entrepreneur offers something—a product or service. You don't have to accept it. It is a voluntary transaction. It encourages cooperation."

George Gilder's influential Reagan-era bestseller *Wealth and Poverty* similarly traced the character-building aspects of capitalism. The mechanisms of the market "neutralize greed," because even the most selfish individuals are forced to find ways of ad-

"A STAKE IN THE WELL-BEING OF OTHER PEOPLE"

Steve Forbes argues that pursuit of profit not only improves the character of the individual but also uplifts the character of society. "Capitalism not only brings about trust and cooperation, but also rewards sharing.... So it's not greed. Greed means 'Me first.' In democratic capitalism, misers don't found the Wal-Marts, the Microsofts, the Sun Microsystems, the Apple Computers of the world. With capitalism you defer gratification and take risks.... To succeed, you need discipline, especially when you're founding a new business. It promotes thriftiness, it promotes sacrifice, it promotes creativity, and you have to have faith in the future.... Democratic capitalism and the spirit of free enterprise also mean you have a stake in the well-being of other people. If others are more prosperous, they can buy more of what you're offering. It's not a zero-sum game. Henry Ford understood this when he established his five-dollar-a-day wage. He understood that if working people had the means they could buy what he was offering. Again, we take it for granted, but it's a marvel of human history" (Heritage Foundation Leadership America Lecture, "Enterprise," September 28, 1998, San Francisco).

dressing the needs of those with whom they wish to exchange. Gilder also demonstrated the way capitalism reinforces the biblical view of man's fallen nature: the market system recognizes the weakness and limitations of human beings and affirms the idea that no one individual (or even a select group) can be entrusted to run a complex economy. Socialism, on the other hand, requires leaders of Godlike purity, wisdom, and restraint to make decisions on behalf of the hapless, befuddled masses.

The public will turn to such "enlightened" and omnipotent authority figures only at moments of intense insecurity and doubt. For instance, at a time of rapidly rising gas prices in 2007, a Wall Street Journal–NBC News poll indicated that more than 90 percent of Americans said they wanted Congress to force the auto companies (even before the government take-over) to build more fuel-efficient cars. If nine out of ten Americans really preferred high-mileage vehicles, why would they need bureaucrats to force them to make an enlightened purchase? The respondents seemed unaware that the market already offered a great many fuel-efficient cars, with obvious economic benefits (and even some tax breaks) for anyone who chose to buy them. But the survey seemed to suggest that the people simply didn't trust themselves: unless the government somehow limited their choices, they couldn't count on their own judgment to produce the right decisions for their wallets, for the environment, and for the country. At one painful point, with a financial crisis looming and a gloomy mood already afflicting the populace, most of the people seemed to trust federal officials to compel the right moves more than they counted on their own positive behavior.

UTTERLY UNSHAKEN BY THE GLOBAL CRISIS

Despite the fears and confusion associated with the economic crisis, the American public hasn't shifted in its fundamentally positive view of the free-market system and its deep doubts about big government. Michael Barone of the American Enterprise Institute noted a June 2009 Washington Post–ABC poll that showed Americans favoring smaller government with fewer services to larger government with more services. The margin was a surprisingly solid 54 to 41 percent—a slightly larger spread than in 2008. The June Wall Street Journal–NBC News poll indicated that even in the midst of deep recession, 58 percent gave priority to holding down the budget deficit, as opposed to only 35 percent who worried most about boosting the economy. Barone observes that "a similar question in the June CBS–New York Times poll showed a 52 percent to 41 percent split. . . . The $787 billion stimulus package, the cap-and-trade bill's utility rate increases, the public health insurance package—all these seem to generate more apprehension than enthusiasm. . . . Americans seem to be recoiling against big government when it threatens to become a reality rather than a campaign promise."

A Gallup poll (April 20, 2009) certainly indicated the same concerns about the growth in federal power. The pollsters asked, "In your opinion, which of the following will be the biggest threat to the country in the future—big business, big labor, or big government?" A surprising 55 percent named "big government," and another 10 percent named government's allies in Big Labor. These numbers mean that fully 65 percent of the public sees either Big Government or Big Labor as a grave threat, while only 32 percent pointed the accusing finger at Big Business—a remarkably low figure following a full year of bank collapses, bailouts, corporate takeovers, and general unrest.

At the same time (April 24, 2009), David Brooks wrote in the *New York Times,*

Americans have always felt that they are masters of their own fate. Decade after decade, Americans stand out from others in their belief that their own individual actions determine how they fare. That conviction has been utterly unshaken by the global crisis. . . . I look at the data and conclude that the tumult has not significantly changed the way Americans look at government, corporations or the social contract. Americans are open to good ideas from government, as always, but they are still skeptical and fiercely self-sufficient. The economic crisis has produced a desire for change, but not a philosophical shift.

BACK ON RECOVERY ROAD?

That kind of consistent, arguably courageous individualism at a time of national insecurity and occasional hysteria may explain the determination even in politically correct Seattle for harried commuters to stay in their cars and to resist the blandishments of the criminally costly Sound Transit light rail system. Nothing promotes a sense of freedom more powerfully than an automobile with a full gas tank, providing an unrivaled ability to take chronically restless Americans wherever they choose to go.

In a misleading attempt to link the new Central Link trains to the rugged, pioneer past of the Great Northwest, some of the expensive propaganda for the fresh system invokes memories of "good old days" with a nostalgic transit timeline, complete with sepia-toned historic pictures:

"1884—Frank Osgood's horse drawn streetcars begin running in Seattle

"1887—First cable cars begin service in Seattle

"1889—First electric streetcars in Seattle

"1890—Westlake streetcar line begins . . ."

and so forth.

Unfortunately, in their eagerness to establish an apostolic transit succession all the way from horse-drawn streetcars to the $2.4 billion light rail train, they forgot to mention that all those earlier efforts to move people from place to place came into existence as private, entrepreneurial, for-profit enterprises and never demanded tax money to launch them. Though the government played no role in instituting the pioneer transportation services, it did have a hand at killing them off. By 1910, twenty-five independent transit lines crisscrossed Seattle, but the ambitious Seattle Electric Company wanted to move into the train and streetcar business and to consolidate all available operations. The resulting corporate giant—known as the Puget Sound Traction, Light and Power Company—began operating in 1912, when a nickel fare took you anywhere. The politicians looked enviously at this bustling business and inevitably decided to take it over: the city bought out Puget Sound Traction in 1919 for $15 million (less than what Sound Transit has spent so far on light rail *publicity*). City management proved disastrous from the beginning—coming up with a confusing fare increase that promised "three rides for a quarter" (or an awkward single fare of eight and a third cents). By 1923, the once-profitable company was running chronic losses and the system itself began to deteriorate at the same time that the exploding popularity of the automobile took away potential riders.

The current effort to lure those drivers back to trains from their indomitable enjoyment of their cars and highways looks both dumb and doomed after Central Link's first week of operation: all media outlets reported less than half-full train cars at peak hours, and nearly empty trains at all other times. This prodigiously wasteful transit experiment is working no better, in other words, than all those other grand schemes that arise from reflexive faith in big-government solutions to every human problem. The bureaucratic impulse to herd all pliant citizens into the same crowded cars doesn't stem from a deep desire to help them but arises rather from an overwhelming need to supervise them—for their own good, of course. Free-market success requires that the businessman shape himself and his enterprise to suit the customers' requirements, but government prevails by trying to force balky citizens into fitting the demands of planners and bureaucrats.

If transit deliverance comes eventually to this "Emerald City" of Seattle, it will arrive as the old streetcars did—with innovations brought to town by adventurous entrepreneurs more eager for profit than official approval. Sure, our city and our national economy will eventually get back on recovery road, but when they do and we begin to gather speed, it's wrong to assume that this empire of individualism will ever see us all barreling along in exactly the same direction.

Lemonade in the Woods

UNEQUIVOCALLY VALUABLE
TO SOMEBODY ELSE

On the way home from work on a summer afternoon, I pulled over to do business with a group of young entrepreneurs who had set up their temporary enterprise not far from our house. On the edge of a forest preserve and in the shadow of towering Douglas firs, four excited little girls dispensed lemonade in

225

plastic cups, along with home-baked cookies contributed by their moms. They appeared to range in age from seven to about twelve, and the two younger girls waved at passing motorists to call attention to the colorful, hand-lettered cardboard signs on three sides of the card table that constituted their base of operations. The older children sat on folding chairs, handling customers, emphasizing the difference between a small cup for fifty cents and a large cup for just a quarter more. They collected their money in a shoe box and the presence of numerous dollar bills along with all the quarters and dimes suggested a productive and successful day of work.

As I completed my transaction and sipped the ice-cold refreshment, I told the budding capitalists that I used to run my own lemonade stands when I was a kid, and so did our three children when they were younger. To my disappointment, the girls didn't seem to hear me: they were already concentrating on other customers who'd been waiting their turn, and in any event they seemed so thrilled with their afternoon's endeavor that they probably preferred to believe that they had personally invented the street corner lemonade business. To them, the experience seemed fresh and exciting rather than timeless and nostalgic.

Nevertheless, they almost certainly shared some of the common characteristics of youthful lemonade vendors of prior generations. For one thing, the children who participate in this neighborhood rite seldom focus on the money they produce. I'm proud to say that our daughters always designated all proceeds to charity, selecting various causes that benefited children with cancer. The enjoyment of the process never stems from the coins or bills collected in the shoe box but from the genial, generous connections with friends, neigh-

LEMONADE VERSUS BUREAUCRACY

When government attempts to crush or corral the entrepreneurial impulse, sometimes the bureaucrats are forced to give way—as they did when they tried to shut down an eight-year-old entrepreneur in Tulare, California, in August 2009. Daniela Earnest hoped to earn money for a family trip to Disneyland, so her stepmother helped her prepare fresh-squeezed lemonade priced at $2 for a 32-ounce plastic cup. The same day that she opened her little business at a major intersection, a city code enforcer happened on the scene to take down some unauthorized signs advertising tetherball poles. Seeing Daniela's lemonade stand, the local official determined it wasn't safe and she lacked a business license, so he quickly helped the girl and her stepmother shut down and disassemble their operation. Inevitably, the case became a controversy on local radio, with the station providing the money for the Earnest family to make their trip to Disneyland. The vice mayor also announced a potential compromise to avoid unnecessary confrontations: in honor of Daniela, the city would consider a "license fee waiver" for children below a certain age so that future eight-year-olds would be allowed to sell refreshing drinks at street corners without official regulation by the city.

bors, and even strangers. When you give a cold drink to a passing patron and he hands you money in return, it's an indication that an adult is taking you seriously, transacting business as an equal.

You've done something useful and the payment confirms that your customer appreciates it. It's also hugely satisfying to serve other people and to watch their pleasure (some of it deliberately exaggerated, no doubt) as they drink your cold lemonade on hot days or savor your cookies. It's the same sort of satisfaction pursued by countless Americans of every age and station (including famous movie actors and sports stars) who nurture the dubious but deathless dream of opening a popular restaurant and drawing mobs of eager, happy diners. Why else would celebrities who already earn tens of millions of dollars risk time, money, and reputation to start steak houses, rib joints, or high-end bar-and-grills? That thrill of building a business, of creating an enduring institution that others will patronize and cherish, provides emotional and even spiritual (if not financial) rewards distinct from the evanescent glories of throwing touchdowns or starring in comedy blockbusters.

The commercial impulse to trade service to others for financial reward remains virtually unquenchable in the human spirit, and will triumph inevitably over all those who celebrate or lament "the death of capitalism" with each new economic crisis. Banks may crumble and investments may tumble (to paraphrase Ira Gershwin) but the entrepreneurial impulse is here to stay. Even in sour economic circumstances, kids will still want to sell sweet lemonade on summer days and their parents will dream of creating some business or another that may make them famous, appreciated, or, very simply, useful. People feel a deep need to make money not just for the options and opportunities the dollars can provide, but as a signal that they've done something that's unequivocally valuable to somebody else.

THE UNQUENCHABLE URGE

At a time of economic hardship, that desire to create wealth through the business system seems to increase as a result of both practical and psychological factors. Experts see a sharp increase in small business start-ups at the depths of the present downturn, in part because workers who have lost their jobs and find it difficult to get rehired will feel ready to strike out on their own, and in part because the unpredictability and shakiness among even the largest corporations encourage venturesome souls to take control of their own circumstances. If all work positions look uncertain and insecure, according to one line of reasoning, you might as well toil yourself as at some remote company.

Surprisingly enough, the rigors of the recession have increased rather than diminished the number of students pursuing graduate educations in business. Despite widespread cutbacks in educational funding for most universities, MBA programs showed explosive growth in applications in 2009. One typical headline (from the *Orlando Business Journal*) proclaimed "MBA Enrollment Spikes as Economic Woes Mount." Meanwhile, *Business Wire* (January 31, 2009) reported from the other side of the country, "Mirroring a national trend, applications to the University of California Davis Graduate School of Management's two-year Daytime MBA program are up 50 percent from last year, the school's admission office reports." These applicants include some laid-off workers who seek new qualifications before reentering the workforce, as well as worried undergraduates who conclude they need more than a BA to get a decent position in a struggling economy. Nevertheless, the growing eagerness to concentrate on business as a field for advanced study shows that many young people emphatically reject the conventional wisdom that capitalism's fate is dire or, at best, cramped. The growing popularity of business degrees among university students, even at a time when scholarships and loans have become more difficult to secure, amounts to an unexpected vote of confidence in the market economy from the hippest, most future-oriented segment of the population.

The yen to build wealth in a market economy not only survives every sort of economic crisis and business scandal but also endures the most ferocious attempts at political repression. The Cultural Revolution in China raged from 1966 to 1976 and represented one of history's most savage efforts to uproot and obliterate the business instinct. Literally millions of those identified as "class enemies," "revisionists," or "running dogs" suffered violent attack, imprisonment, torture, rape, confiscation of property, and execution. Senior Communist Party historians now acknowledge that "in a few places, it even happened that 'counterrevolutionaries' were beaten to death and in the most beastly fashion had their flesh and liver consumed by their killers." The most authoritative estimates of the number of murder victims suggest 500,000 in the years 1966–69 alone—a total collection of corpses easily exceeding in number the well-publicized hordes who partied at the Woodstock Festival in 1969. Nevertheless, a quarter century later the Chinese regime not only tolerated but celebrated the same business values and pursuit of profit that had formerly provoked unspeakable persecution and even mass cannibalism. As the brilliant French journalist and academic Guy Sorman observes in his latest book, *Economics Does Not Lie* (2009), "It is a remarkable historical event that the largest coun-

try in the world, under the guidance of a Party that tried to rein-
vent economics from scratch in the 1960s, has admitted that,
after all, there is only one economic system that works: the market economy."

While others might claim that the survival of business values
in China stems from the long national tradition of honoring
merchants and artisans, Sorman asserts that the impulse to seek
profit and self-improvement is entirely transnational. "After
banishing the pursuit of wealth for fifty years," he writes, "the
Party now encourages it. It is once again permissible in China to
work in order to make money. Indeed, this is the only authorized and encouraged activity. We see that the Chinese have the
same aspirations as other peoples. From the poor peasant to the
dynamic entrepreneur, everyone wants to improve his lot and
that of his children. The *homo economicus* is a universal being,
found in all civilizations."

The Soviet Empire in Eastern Europe may have shed even
more blood in its futile efforts to wipe out that "universal
being." The Nobel Prize–winning novelist and historian Alek-
sandr Solzhenitsyn suggested that some 60 million kulaks, or
independent farmers, died at the hands of Lenin and Stalin for
the crime of working for themselves rather than the state; official Soviet-era low-range estimates say "only" 700,000 met their
doom. In any event, the survivors and heirs of that nightmare
regime now coexist with an aggressive business elite more flamboyant, corrupt, and ambitious than the most notorious captains of industry in America's Gilded Age.

Just five years after the collapse of the old Soviet Union and
the new independence of its onetime satellite states, I traveled to
Warsaw for a lecture to an international media conference at the
Palace of Culture and Science. This monstrous building, the

tallest in Poland and the eighth-tallest in the European Union, has dominated the local skyline since its construction began in 1952, and it sprawls over four square blocks with its various wings and subdivisions. Originally known as the "Joseph Stalin Palace of Culture and Science," it featured a special throne room from which later Soviet dictators could watch the proceedings of Communist Party congresses that convened regularly in the Congress Hall.

By 1994, the Poles had discovered the best possible way to insult Stalin's evil ghost. Every day a veritable army of peddlers and merchants surrounded the palace, setting up literally thousands of booths to sell every sort of merchandise, from shoes to food to cameras to wigs to cigarettes to pirated CDs to traditional handicrafts. The intense haggling exemplified capitalism in an especially vital, even elemental form; after nearly fifty years of ideological efforts to suppress these instincts, the mobs around Stalin's former Palace reveled in their newfound ability to buy and sell.

The people of every age who came out every day to sell all manner of junk in 1990s Warsaw didn't intend to make a self-conscious, pro-capitalist statement, or have the expectation that they'd get rich. They seized the chance to do business in the public square to earn a few zlotys, and to savor the festive communal atmosphere and the unstoppable energy of that moment in their history.

BUILDING RELATIONSHIPS

My own singular adventure in ground-level business building similarly stemmed from a lust for personal adventure and experimentation rather than any conscious commitment to a free-market agenda. At age seventeen, in the summer of 1966, having completed my freshman year at Yale, I needed to earn some serious money for my continued education to supplement my parents' contribution and my National Merit Scholarship. I initially used the university's alumni association to secure a minimum-wage bank job near my family's home in West L.A., but my boredom in the institution's copy room quickly led to disaster. I liked to play around with the bank's bulky, primitive Xerox machine, trying to produce some artistic photographic collages, but managed during my second week of employment to set the contraption on fire. The resulting blaze did no serious damage to the building but it definitely ended my banking career and led to desperation regarding my wealth-generating prospects for the rest of the summer.

Rather than doing nothing while I checked the want ads, I paid an unauthorized visit to an American history class at the summer session at UCLA and quickly devised a scheme to try to sell notes and "study guides" to the more than 500 students who attended the lectures. I took class notes in the morning, walked over to the library to type them up on master mimeograph sheets (in a barbaric era long before the advent of laptops), and then made enough copies to hand out to every student in the class during the first week. At the bottom of the thorough notes I also began a countdown till the end of the free notes, hoping that the bulk of the huge class would become so addicted to my services that they'd buy a subscription to my newly launched company, Stratford Study Guides (named for the Bard of Avon, and the classy Anglophiliac sound of the designation).

Everything worked beautifully and I began to sell subscriptions, but the entire scheme came close to collapse when the professor (very reasonably) objected. He could have thrown me out of the lecture hall, since I'd never registered to attend or even audited his course, but instead he merely protested that my virtually word-for-word transcriptions of his talks violated his copyright and led students to ignore him, since they could count on my very detailed notes. To settle the dispute, I suggested that Stratford Study Guides become real study guides— still transcribing his lectures more or less verbatim but leaving at least four blanks in each sentence that the students would need to fill in for themselves. For instance, I might report that "to support the ratification of the Constitution, _____, James Madison, and _____ wrote a series of brilliantly argumentative essays known as _____."

The lecturer loved (and, more important, authorized) the new approach, and by the middle of the summer term the overwhelming majority of students in the class had purchased one of my subscriptions. By working frantically and constantly (I can still smell the sharp alcohol tang of the master mimeograph sheets and recall their slimy feel), I managed to hand out the previous day's lecture notes to all subscribers (as I punched their cards) at the conclusion of every daily lecture. I also began offering tutoring services (at the suggestion of some of my customers) to assist in preparation for midterms and finals. These personalized sessions led to a brief but thrilling summer romance (unfortunately not with my future wife, Diane, who was still a child at the time and didn't start UCLA till years later).

The summer's experiment with Stratford Study Guides did wonders for my self-confidence, selling ability, historical knowledge, and bank account. As the term came to an end and I prepared to return to New Haven, several satisfied customers and even the initially dubious professor approached me as potential investors with the idea of perpetuating and expanding my little business. If I stayed behind at UCLA, why not replicate my successful formula in other large lecture courses by hiring a group of note-takers who could prepare study guides at my direction? Perhaps I could make some deal with the university bookstore to help distribute the lecture-based material, plus other student aids that I could generate to help prepare for tests and even term papers.

In one sense, I loved the idea of staying back in California and building my own business, but my mother persuaded me that it made no sense to suspend my own college education so I could help other students make easier progress toward *their* degrees. I did hope to keep "my company" (there was no incorporation or anything of the kind) going until I could resume directing its operations the following summer, so I sold it to a friend of mine with the understanding that he'd continue running Stratford Study Guides in some capacity. I believe the purchase price for my going concern amounted to the princely fee of $50, which ended up as a total waste for the new tycoon, who quickly abandoned the whole effort because of lack of focus as his UCLA course demands intensified.

Like my mom, my father wanted me to return to Yale, but he watched my business develop with particularly keen interest. He had begun plotting to leave his corporate and government jobs to open his own high-tech business providing "hybrid opto-electronic devices"—a far more sophisticated line of products than mimeographed lecture notes. Within three years, he'd successfully launched MERET (Medved Research and Technology), and then my kid brother Jonathan also caught the entrepreneurial bug. At the University of California, Berkeley, he enjoyed conspicuous success with a company called "Meshuggeneh Brothers"—even though none of his real life *meshuga* (crazy) brothers managed to help him with it. He delivered overstuffed, overpriced deli sandwiches he made from food he bought in bulk to dorm rooms and frat houses at Cal to help fortify his fellow students who needed nourishment during late-night study. Jonathan has gone on to build a fruitful and internationally recognized career as a venture capitalist in Israel.

In all of these oddly assorted family enterprises we certainly hoped to make money, but like most others inspired by the romance and adventure of business, we also looked for other sorts of pay—for my father, the respect (and in fact awe) of his physicist colleagues when he turned out products they deemed impossible to produce, for Jon the grateful joy of a hungry dorm-bound fellow student lighting into a huge, freshly prepared pastrami and rye at two in the morning before a major test, and for me the heart-fluttering experience of offering a tutoring session about Henry Clay, Daniel Webster, and the Great Compromise of 1850 while a buxom California coed listened with rapt attention and dewy, admiring eyes.

Business, even in its most rudimentary sense, builds more than profits—it builds relationships.

BRINGING ORDER OUT OF CHAOS

The importance of those relationships intensifies during periods of financial turmoil and uncertainty, helping to explain the stubborn survival of the business ethos through every crisis and challenge. "Considerable courage and perseverance are required to start and keep a good shop running," writes Joseph Epstein of

OUTLASTING LENIN'S CREATION

Bertie Charles Forbes, the founder of the Forbes empire in communications and journalism, was the sixth of ten children and never got beyond the sixth grade in school. He immigrated to the United States at age twenty-four from Scotland (after a brief sojourn in South Africa) and became famous for his punchy aphorisms, sound financial advice, and infectious enthusiasm for the American business system. Some of his more popular quotations:

"Sweat makes sweet."

"Strive to become the kind of pal that doesn't pall."

"Any business arrangement that is not profitable to the other person will in the end prove unprofitable for you. The bargain that yields mutual satisfaction is the only one that is apt to be repeated."

"You make more money selling the advice than following it."

"Work is the meat of life, pleasure the desert."

His grandson and successor as head of the magazine, Steve Forbes, recalled, "My grandfather founded Forbes back in 1917, the same year as the Russian Revolution—and wherever my grandfather is he must be delighted that his creation outlasted Lenin's creation."

Northwestern University. In responding to Napoleon's ill-considered dismissal of the British as a "nation of shopkeepers," Epstein extolled the skill and determination required to "keep shop," reminding me that even my dad, with his several dozen employees, referred to his fiber optics company as his "shop." As

Epstein wrote (in the *Wall Street Journal,* July 16, 2009), "Running a good shop is a service to one's community, of much greater value, in my view, than the work of two hundred social workers, five hundred psychotherapists, and a thousand second-rate poets—and more honorable than the efforts of the vast majority of the members of Congress. A nation of shopkeepers, far from being the put-down Napoleon thought, sounds more and more like an ideal to which a healthy country ought to aspire."

That aspiration to build and defend businesses arises from the very core of our humanity and for many Americans involves an important religious component. One of the most famous of all Bible verses (Genesis 1:27) declares, "So God created Man in His image, in the image of God he created him." Jewish sages have never understood the reference to connote a physical resemblance between man and God, but rather to emphasize the Godlike gift of creativity. As the Creator busies Himself eternally with the business of constant making and shaping, bringing order out of chaos (a universe once "formless and void"), so human beings, in His likeness, feel the constant urge to create, to connect and organize.

This creative urge gave rise to capitalism, with artisans and craftsmen (who used their own divine power to shape precious things with their hands) playing a decisive role. Historians often cite the thirteenth-century development of the Hanseatic League in northern Europe along the Baltic and North Sea as the beginnings of the medieval mercantile system. Certainly, goldsmiths (who skillfully shaped the most precious of metals according to their will) became the first bankers, making clear the creative essence of a modern financial system.

The current system will adjust to its shocks and catastrophes and continue to create, harnessing the God-given impulse of humans everywhere. Fareed Zakaria of *Newsweek* put the turmoil in an appropriate perspective: "What we are experiencing is not a crisis of capitalism. It is a crisis of finance, of democracy, of globalization and ultimately of ethics," he writes. "The simple truth is that with all its flaws, capitalism remains the most productive economic engine we have yet invented. Like Churchill's line about democracy, it is the worst of all economic systems, except for the others."

On a more ebullient note, Bertie Charles Forbes (1880–1954), the Scottish immigrant founder of *Forbes* magazine, once memorably declared, "Business was originated to produce happiness."

To *produce* happiness perhaps, but to *pursue* it—most certainly.

Resources

Books

Aguiar, Mark and Erik Hurst. *The Increase in Leisure Inequality 1965–2005.* Washington, DC: The AEI Press, 2009.

Bhagwati, Jagdish. *In Defense of Globalization.* New York: Oxford University Press USA, 2004.

Bierce, Ambrose. *The Collected Works of Ambrose Bierce,* vol. 9. New York and Washington: Neale Publishing Company, 1911.

———. *The Devil's Dictionary.* Charlotte, NC: IAP, 2008.

Broda, Christian and David E. Weinstein. *Prices, Poverty and Inequality: Why Americans Are Better Off Than You Think.* Washington, DC: The AIE Press, 2008.

Brooks, Arthur C. *Gross National Happiness: Why Happiness Matters for America and How We Can Get More of It.* New York: Basic Books, 2008.

Caplow, Theodore, Louis Hicks, and Ben J. Wattenberg. *The First Measured Century: An Illustrated Guide to Trends in America, 1900–2000.* Washington, DC: The AEI Press, 2001.

Collins, Jim. *Good to Great.* New York: HarperBusiness, 2001.

DeMint, Jim. *Saving Freedom: We Can Stop America's Slide into Socialism.* Nashville, TN: Fidelis Books, 2009.

Dennis, Lawrence. *The Coming of American Fascism: The Crisis of Capitalism.* Newport Beach, CA: Noontide Press, 1993.

———. *Is Capitalism Doomed?* New York: Harper & Brothers, 1932.

Dickens, Charles. *A Christmas Carol.* New York: Random House, 1990.

DiLorenzo, Thomas J. *How Capitalism Saved America.* New York: Three Rivers Press, 2004.

Dobbs, Lou. *War on the Middle Class: How the Government, Big Business and Special Interest Groups Are Waging War on the American Dream and How to Fight Back.* New York: Viking Penguin, 2006.

D'Souza, Dinesh. *Ronald Reagan: How an Ordinary Man Became an Extraordinary Leader.* New York: Free Press, 1997.

Epstein, Rabbi Isidore. *The Babylonian Talmud.* London: Soncino Press, 1935.

Fitzgerald, F. Scott. *The Great Gatsby.* New York: Scribner Book Company, 1996.

Folsom, Burton W. *The Myth of the Robber Barons: A New Look at the Rise of Big Business in America.* Herndon, VA: Young America's Foundation, 1993.

Friedman, George. *The Next 100 Years: A Forecast for the 21st Century.* New York: Doubleday, 2009.

Gilder, George. *The Spirit of Enterprise.* New York: Simon & Schuster, 1984.

———. *Wealth and Poverty.* New York: ICS Press, 1993.

Gordon, John Steele. *An Empire of Wealth: The Epic History of American Economic Power.* New York: HarperCollins, 2004.

Graham, Edward M. *Fighting the Wrong Enemy: Antiglobal Activists and Multinational Enterprises.* Washington, DC: Institute for International Economics, 2004.

Hemingway, Ernest. *The Snows of Kilimanjaro and Other Stories.* New York: Scribner Book Company, 1995.

Klein, Naomi. *The Shock Doctrine: The Rise of Disaster Capitalism.* New York: Henry Holt & Co., 2007.

Laffer, Arthur B., PhD, Stephen Moore, and Peter J. Tanous. *The End of Prosperity: How Higher Taxes Will Doom the Economy—If We Let It Happen.* New York: Threshold Editions, 2008.

Lapin, Rabbi Daniel. *Thou Shall Prosper: Ten Commandments for Making Money.* Hoboken, NJ: John Wiley & Sons, 2002.

Lewis, Sinclair. *Babbitt.* Mineola, NY: Dover Publications, 2003.

Lichter, Robert S., Linda S. Lichter, and Stanley Rothman. *Prime Time: How TV Portrays American Culture.* Washington, DC: Regnery Publishing, 1993.

Lott, John R. *Freedomnomics: Why the Free Market Works and Other Half-Baked Theories Don't.* Washington, DC: Regenery Publishing, 2007.

Meacham, Jon. *American Lion: Andrew Jackson in the White House.* New York: Random House, 2008.

Medved, Michael. *Hollywood vs. America.* New York: HarperCollins, 1992.

Miller, Arthur. *Death of a Salesman.* New York: Penguin Group, 1976.

Podhoretz, Norman. *Why Are Jews Liberal?* New York: Doubleday, 2009.

Rand, Ayn. *Atlas Shrugged.* New York: Random House, 1957.

———. *Capitalism: The Unknown Ideal.* New York: Signet Books, 1986.

Richards, Jay W. *Money, Greed and God: Why Capitalism Is the Solution and Not the Problem.* New York: HaperOne, 2009.

Roth, Philip. *Goodbye, Columbus.* New York: Vintage Books USA, 1994.

Rothbard, Murray. *Man, Economy, and State.* Auburn, AL: Ludwig von Mises Institute, 1993.

Samuelson, Robert. *The Great Inflation and Its Aftermath: The Past and Future of American Affluence.* New York: Random House, 2008.

Scheiber, Harry N. *United States Economic History: Selected Readings.* New York: Alfred A. Knopf, 1964.

Scherman, Nosson. *The Chumash: The Stone Edition.* New York: Mesorah Publications, Limited, 1999.

Schiff, Peter D. with John Downes. *Crash Proof: How to Profit from the Coming Economic Collapse.* Hoboken, NJ: John Wiley & Sons, 2007.

Shane, Scott. *The Illusions of Entrepreneurship: The Costly Myths That Entrepreneurs, Investors, and Policy Makers Live By.* New Haven: Yale University Press, 2008.

Shlaes, Amity. *The Forgotten Man.* New York: HarperCollins, 2007.

Smith, Adam. *The Wealth of Nations.* New York: Prometheus Books, 1991.

Sorman, Guy. *Economics Does Not Lie: A Defense of the Free Market in a Time of Crisis.* New York/London: Encounter Books, 2009.

Sowell, Thomas. *Basic Economics: A Citizen's Guide to the Economy.* New York: Basic Books, 2000.

Wallis, Jim. *God's Politics: Why the Right Gets It Wrong and the Left Doesn't Get It.* San Francisco: HarperSan Francisco, 2006.

Woods, Thomas E. *Meltdown: A Free Market Look at Why the Stock Market Collapsed, the Economy Tanked and Government Bailouts Will Make Things Worse.* Washington, DC: Regnery Publishing, 2009.

ARTICLES, SPEECHES, AND SONGS

"200–300 Bodies Disinterred in Grave-Reselling Scheme." *Seattle Times,* July 10, 2009.

"44% Believe Constitution Doesn't Restrict Government Enough." Rasmussen Reports (Rasmussenreports.com), June 10, 2009.

"A Brief History of the Cable Cars." Streetcar.org, retrieved June 2009.

Ahrens, Frank. "A 'Manchurian' Capstone to Movies' Hate Affair with Corporations." *Washington Post,* August 8, 2004.

"American Capitalism Gone with a Whimper." Pravda.ru, April 27, 2009.

"Analyzing Economic Mobility: Measuring Inequality and Economic Mobility: Web Memo No. 1478." The Heritage Foundation, May 31, 2007.

Anderson, Jeffrey H., PhD. "Government Care Costs More." *New York Post,* July 18, 2009.

Anderson, Scott. "What's a CEO Worth?" *University of Toronto Magazine,* Summer 2009.

Anderson, William L. "The Income Inequality Hoax." *Mises Daily,* March 10, 2000.

Angur, Madhukar. "Executive Pay Isn't That Excessive and Some CEO's Really Deserve It." *Investor's Business Daily* (IBDeditorials.com), March 23, 2009.

Archibold, Randal C. "Fans Rally, and Officials Brace to Honor Jackson." *New York Times,* July 4, 2009.

Arnoldy, Ben and Brad Knickerbocker. "Video Games, Gas Prices Cut Traffic to US Parks." *The Christian Science Monitor,* May 25, 2007.

"Bacon Hunt: Stimulus Bill Contains Many Items That May Not Boost Economy." Foxnews.com, February 12, 2009.

Bakshian, Aram, Jr. "The Spirit of Enterprise." *National Review,* February 8, 1985.

Balko, Radley. "Altruism? Bah, Humbug." The Cato Institute (Cato.org), December 22, 2004.

Barnes, Fred. "An Anti-Business President." *The Weekly Standard,* June 22, 2009.

Barone, Michael. "Getting Cold Feet over Big Government." Real Clear Politics (Realclearpolitics.com), July 9, 2009.

Barra, Allen. "Sports Salaries Show What We Really Value." *Wall Street Journal,* July 1, 2009.

Bartlett, Bruce. "How Outsourcing Creates Jobs for America." National Center for Policy Analysis (Ncpa.org), July 27, 2004.

Bebchuk, Lucian. "Congress Gets Punitive on Executive Pay." *Wall Street Journal,* February 17, 2009.

Beckel, Bob and Cal Thomas. "Is This Class Warfare?" *USA Today,* April 16, 2009.

Bellamy, John Foster. "The End of Rational Capitalism." *Monthly Review* (Monthlyreview.org), March 2005.

Bittinger, Cyndy. "The Business of America Is Business?" The Calvin Coolidge Memorial Foundation (Calvin-coolidge.org), retrieved June 29, 2009.

Bittlingmayer, George and Thomas W. Hazlett. "FDR's Conservative 100 Days." *Wall Street Journal,* March 19, 2009.

Blinder, Alan S. "Crazy Compensation and the Crisis." *Wall Street Journal,* May 28, 2009.

Bohlen, Celestine. "Use of French Terrorism Law on Railroad Saboteurs Draws Criticism." *New York Times,* November 4, 2008.

Bond, Sharon. "U.S. Charitable Giving Estimates to Be $307.65 Billion in 2008." Giving USA Foundation, June 10, 2009.

Brand, Constant and Robert Wielaard. "Conservatives Racing Ahead in EU Parliament Voting." Associated Press, June 7, 2009.

Brinkley, Alan. "Railing Against the Rich: A Great American Tradition." *Wall Street Journal,* February 7, 2009.

Brooks, Arthur C. "The Left's 'Inequality' Obsession." *Wall Street Journal,* July 19, 2007.

———. "The Real Culture Is over Capitalism." *Wall Street Journal,* April 30, 2009.

———. "Where's the Outrage? Really." *Wall Street Journal,* July 31, 2006.

———. "Why We're Happy." *Reader's Digest,* June 16, 2008.

Brooks, David. "The Gang System." *New York Times,* February 6, 2009.

———. "In Praise of Dullness." *New York Times,* May 19, 2009.

———. "Yanks in Crisis." *New York Times,* April 25, 2009.

Bryan, William Jennings. Cross of Gold Speech. Chicago, July 9, 1896.

Buchholz, Todd G. "There Is No Upside to a Down Economy." *Wall Street Journal,* June 5, 2009.

"Capitalism: RIP." Politics et Cetera. The Political Forum LLC, February 2, 2009.

Carey, Anne R. and K. A. Kepple. "Bubbles Burst: Views on Sour Economy." *USA Today,* April 27, 2009.

Carr, David. "Hit by the Recession, Even Forbes Is Pinching Pennies." *New York Times,* June 15, 2009.

———. "Unhealthy Fixation on Jobs's Illness." *New York Times,* July 6, 2009.

Cato, Jeremy. "10 Best Buys." *The Globe and Mail* (Theglobeandmail.com), May 5, 2009.

"Changes in the Economic Resources of Low-Income Households with Children." Pub. No. 2602, Congress of the United States, Congressional Budget Office, May 2007.

Chaplin, Ralph. "Solidarity Forever." Lyrics. 1914.

Cho, David. "Bailout Money May Be Used to Bolster Small Business." *Washington Post*, July 11, 2009.

Clarridge, Christine. "No Charges in Slamming Case." *Seattle Times*, August 1, 2009.

Clegg, Roger. "Roger Clegg Reviews *America in Black and White*, by Stephen and Abigail Thernstrom." Civil Rights Group Newsletter, May 1, 1998.

Collins, William W. "Mandate Altruism from Executives." *Business Week*, June 25, 2008.

Colvin, Geoff. "Higher Taxes for Business Mean We All Pay." *Washington Post*, June 30, 2009.

Conley, Dalton. "The Rich Man's Burden." *New York Times*, September 2, 2008.

Coolidge, Calvin. "The Press Under a Free Government." Address Before the American Society of Newspaper Editors, Washington, DC, January 17, 1925.

Corcoran, Elizabeth. "Tech's Top-Paid CEOs." *Forbes*, May 2, 2008.

Corcoran, Terence. "Is This the End of America?" *National Post*, March 19, 2009.

Coulson, Andrew J. "The Real Cost of Public Schools." *Washington Post*, April 6, 2008.

David, Bob. "World Economies Plummet." *Wall Street Journal*, May 21, 2009.

Davis, Scott. "Business Needs to Speak Up on Trade." *Wall Street Journal*, July 16, 2009.

DeCarlo, Sandy. "What the Boss Makes." *Forbes*, April 22, 2009.

Deeran, Stefan. "Small Business May Not Be the Key to Economic Recovery." Bnet.com, July 2, 2009.

Dionne, E. J., Jr. "President Obama Should Brace for a Capitalist Counteroffensive." *Seattle Times*, June 16, 2009.

Doughton, Sandi and Mike Lindblom. "Seattle Hops on Board." *Seattle Times*, July 19, 2009.

D'Souza, Dinesh. "The Decade of Greed That Wasn't." *Forbes*, November 3, 1997.

Dubner, Stephen J. "Let's Talk About Tax Cheating: A Freakonomics Quorum." *New York Times* Freakanomics Blog, March 27, 2009.

Ennis, Michael. "Light Rail Carries Big Cost, Little Benefit." *The Columbian*, April 25, 2008.

———. "Part IV: Light Rail and Interstate 90." Washington Policy Center (Washingtonpolicy.org), December 2007.

Epstein, Joseph. "In Praise of Shopkeepers." *Wall Street Journal*, July 16, 2009.

Farrell, Greg and Kevin McCoy. "She Stood by Her Man—Until Now." *USA Today*, August 17, 2006.

Fleischer, Ari. "Everyone Should Pay Income Taxes." *Wall Street Journal*, April 13, 2009.

Forbes, Steve. "Enterprise." *San Francisco*, September 28, 1998.

———. "How Capitalism Will Save Us." *Forbes*, November 10, 2008.

Frank, Robert and Amir Efrati. "'Evil' Madoff Gets 150 Years in Epic Fraud." *Wall Street Journal,* June 30, 2009.

Fraser, Steve. "The Specter of Wall Street." Middle East Online (Middle-east-online.com), October 3, 2008.

Friedman, Thomas L. "Make Greenbacks with Green Cards." *Seattle Times,* February 12, 2009.

———. "Obama's Big Bold Bet." *New York Times,* April 5, 2009.

Ferguson, Niall. "Diminished Returns: Why We Never Learn the Right Lessons from Financial Crisis." *New York Times Magazine,* May 15, 2009.

Gauthier-Villars, David and Marcus Walker. "Across Europe, Left-Leaning Parties See Clout Faltering." *Wall Street Journal,* June 6–7, 2009.

Genzlinger, Neil. "That Big Hole in the Economy, and Who Dug It." Television Review. *New York Times,* March 24, 2009.

Goldberg, Jonah. "Don't Call It 'Socialism.'" *USA Today,* June 2, 2009.

Gordon, John Steele. "Read Your History, Janet." *Forbes,* February 23, 1998.

Griswold, Daniel. "Lou Dobbs: The Dan Rather of Financial Journalism." Techcentralstation.com, October 8, 2004.

Gross, Daniel. "No Rest for the Wealthy." Book Review. *New York Times,* July 5, 2009.

———. "The Recession Is Over." *Newsweek,* August 3, 2009.

Gutierrez, Scott. "Crowds Down but Riders Still Taking Light Rail." *Seattle Post-Intelligencer,* July 20, 2009.

Hager, Daniel. "Ambrose Bierce on Socialism." *The Freeman,* December 2004.

Harris Poll #19: "Confidence in Leaders of Major Institutions." Harris Interactive (Harrisinteractive.com), March 1, 2007.

Henchman, Joseph. "Most Americans Say Tax Cheating Is Not Acceptable." The Tax Foundation (Taxfoundation.org), February 6, 2009.

Henderson, David R. "The Rich—and Poor—Are Getting Richer." *Red Herring,* August 1997.

Henninger, Daniel. "Is This the End of Capitalism?" *Wall Street Journal,* April 2, 2009.

Hinderaker, John H. and Scott W. Johnson. "The Truth About Income Inequality." Center of the American Experiment, December 1995.

Hindo, Brian. "Even in Retreat, Jack Welch Leads." *Business Week,* September 18, 2002.

"Historical Income Tables—Households." U.S. Census Bureau, Housing and Household Economic Statistics Division, August 26, 2008.

Hoag, Christina. "Michael Jackson Memorial Cost LA 1.4 Million." Associated Press, July 9, 2009.

Hochenauer, Kurt. "Let Wall Street Die." Okiefunk.com, September 24, 2008.

Hodak, Marc. "Wall Street Deserved Its Bonuses." *Forbes,* February 19, 2009.

Holden, Stephen. "When Laws and Liberties Test Each Other's Limitations." Film Review. *New York Times,* December 3, 2008.

Hornblow, Deborah and Hartford Courant. "Corporations Take an Onscreen Beating." *Los Angeles Times,* August 6, 2004.

Hossli, Peter. "I Am Innocent." Hossli.com, May 2009.

Hudgins, Edward L. "Put Amtrak in Hands of Private Company." *Atlanta Journal Constitution,* September 30, 2003.

Ingrassia, Paul. "The UAW in the Driver's Seat." *Wall Street Journal,* April 30, 2009.

Istook, Ernest. "Government's Comedy of Errors." *Human Events,* July 6, 2009.

Jackson, Andrew. Farewell Address. Washington, DC, March 4, 1837.

———. "Veto Message Regarding the Bank of the United States." Washington, DC, July 10, 1832.

Jimenez, Eddie. "Tulare Put Squeeze on Girl's Lemonade Stand." *Fresno Bee,* August 6, 2009.

Jones, Jeffrey M. "Big Gov't Still Viewed as Greater Threat Than Big Business." Gallup.com, April 20, 2009.

Kane, Tim, Brett D. Schaefer, and Alison Acosta Fraser. "Web Memo # 467: Ten Myths About Jobs and Outsourcing." The Heritage Foundation, April 1, 2004.

Karabell, Zachary. "Washington Has Always Demonized Wall Street." *Wall Street Journal,* March 19, 2009.

Kargianis, George and Phil Talmadge. "The Hidden Cost of Light Rail Across the I-90 Bridge." *Seattle Times,* May 16, 2007.

Kerry, John. "John Kerry Addresses Supporters." New Hampshire, January 27, 2004.

Kilmer, Marc. "Viewpoint: When Government Competes with Private Enterprise, You Pay." The Buckeye Institute for Public Policy Solutions, April 17, 2006.

Kirdahy, Matthew. "America's Most Generous Corporations." *Forbes,* October 16, 2008.

Klass, Tim. "After Decades, Light-Rail Trains Run in Seattle." Associated Press, July 15, 2009.

Krauthammer, Charles. "Obama Seeks Fairness Through Leveling of America." *Deseret News,* April 5, 2009.

Krishnan, Sonia. "Would-Be Rail Riders Bemoan Lack of Parking." *Seattle Times,* July 16, 2009.

Laffer, Arthur B. "Spend It in Vegas or Die Paying Taxes." *Wall Street Journal,* April 2, 2009.

——— and Stephen Moore. "Soak the Rich, Lose the Rich." *Wall Street Journal,* May 18, 2009.

Lange, Larry. "Is Expanding Light Rail Worth the Cost?" *Seattle Post-Intelligencer,* October 31, 2008.

———. "Light Rail's Million Dollar Launch." *Seattle PostGlobe,* July 7, 2009.

Lasky, Ed. "Government Run Health Care More Expensive Than Private Sector Care." *American Thinker,* July 18, 2009.

Leonhardt, David. "The Looting of America's Coffers." *New York Times,* March 11, 2009.

Lewis, Michael and David Einhorn. "The End of the Financial World as We Know It." *New York Times,* January 4, 2009.

Lewis, Sandy B. and William D. Cohan. "The Economy Is Still at the Brink." *New York Times,* June 7, 2009.

Limbaugh, David. "Memo to Capitalists: Be Very Afraid." Townhall.com, May 8, 2009.

Lindsay, C. G. and Rita Gunther McGrath. "We'll Become More Like Europe, with Slower Growth." *Wall Street Journal,* July 21, 2009.

Lips, Dan, Shanea J. Watkins, PhD, and John Fleming. "Does Spending More on Education Improve Academic Achievement?" The Heritage Foundation, September 8, 2008.

Long, Juey and Castro Carazo. "Every Man a King." Lyrics. 1935.

Loungani, Prakash. "Globalization Without Tears." *Reason,* August 2004.

Lowenstein, Roger. "A Seat at the Table." *New York Times Magazine,* June 2, 2009.

Lowry, Brian. "Hollywood Loves to Hate Big Business." *Variety,* July 22, 2008.

Malanga, Steven. "Capitalism and the Cheating Ethic." Real Clear Markets (Realclearmarkets.com), May 20, 2009.

Matthews, Joe. "Democrats for a Flat Tax?" *Wall Street Journal,* July 11–12, 2009.

McCormick, Richard. "10 Myths about Globalization." Speech. Denver, Colorado, September 28, 2000.

Meacham, Jon and Evan Thomas. "We Are All Socialists Now." *Newsweek,* February 16, 2009.

Menefee, Amy. "Bad Company." Special Report. The Business and Media Institute, 2007.

Meredith, Robyn and Suzanne Hoppough. "Why Globalization Is Good." *Forbes,* April 16, 2007.

"MetropoLIST 150: The 150 Most Influential People in Seattle/King County History." *Seattle Times.* Retrieved December 2007.

Miller, Joshua Rhett. " 'Capitalism Will Fail,' Marijuana Leaf Part of California School Mosaic." Fox News (Foxnews.com), June 25, 2009.

Miller, Terry. "Freedom Is Still the Winning Formula." *Wall Street Journal,* January 13, 2009.

Moore, Stephen. "Amtrak Subsidies: This Is No Way to Run a Railroad." Cato.org, May 22, 1997.

———. "Mission Milton: Who Will Speak for Free Markets?" *Wall Street Journal,* May 29, 2009.

Moynihan, Colin. "Liberating Lipsticks and Lattes." *New York Times,* June 16, 2009.

Murakami, Kery. "Seattle's First Electric Streetcar Zipped Up James Street in 1889." *Seattle Post-Intelligencer,* November 17, 2005.

Murphy, Robert. "In Defense of CEO Compensation." Townhall.com, September 15, 2007.

Murray, Alan. "Another Day at the Office: The Truth About Middle Managers." Book Review. *Wall Street Journal,* February 25, 2009.

Mydans, Seth. "Suits Against Critics Rise in Cambodia." *New York Times,* July 21, 2009.

Nader, Ralph. "The Road to Corporate Fascism." Washington, DC, October 6, 2007.

Newport, Frank. "Americans Concerned About Gov't Spending, Expansion." Gallup.com, July 22, 2009.

Niles, John S. "Part III: Costs Exceed Benefits in Sound Transit Light Rail Expansion." Washington Policy Center (Washingtonpolicy.org), October 2007.

Nocera, Joe. "First Let's Fix the Bonuses." *New York Times,* February 21, 2009.

Norris, Floyd. "It May Be Outrageous, but Wall Street Pay Didn't Cause This Crisis." *New York Times,* July 31, 2009.

Noyes, Rich. "Issue Analysis: Big Business vs. Small Business on Prime Time." Media Research Center (Mrc.org), June 1997.

Obama, Barack. Commencement Address at Arizona State University. Phoenix, AZ, May 13, 2009.

"Officials Begin to ID the 100,000 Graves in Burial-Plot Scam." Fox News (Foxnews.com), July 13, 2009.

Ogg, Erica. "Buffett: Apple Should Have Disclosed Jobs' Surgery." CNET News (News.cnet.com), June 24, 2009.

O'Grady, Mary Anastasia. "Now Is No Time to Give Up on Markets." *Wall Street Journal,* March 21, 2009.

O'Keefe, Ed. "Lawmakers to Weigh Postal Overhaul." *Seattle Times,* July 30, 2009.

O'Rourke, P.J. "A Message to Redistributionists." Cato Policy Report, Cato.org, July 2007.

Palmer, Caitriona. "The Enigmatic Genius of Jobs." *The Irish Independent* (Independent.ie), June 27, 2009.

Passel, Jeffrey S. "A Portrait of Unauthorized Immigrants in the United States." Pew Research Center, April 14, 2009.

Pergams, Oliver R. W. and Patricia A. Zaradic. "Is Love of Nature in the US Becoming Love of Electronic Media?" Science Direct (Sciencedirect.com), March 30, 2006.

"Philanthropy Among Corporations and Their Executives." Wachovia Trust Nonprofit and Philanthropic Services, December 15, 2008.

Poor, Jeff. "Capitalism: Pronounced Dead According to CNBC Analyst." Business and Media Institute, September 19, 2008.

———. "Coming to a Theater Near You: Wall Street Villains!" Business and Media Institute, December 30, 2009.

Postrel, Virginia. "The Rich Get Richer and Poor Get Poorer. Or Do They?" *New York Times,* August 15, 2002.

Preston, Caroline. "Corporate Leaders Tout Philanthropy Benefits amid Grim Financial News." *The Chronicle of Philanthropy* (Philanthropy.com), February 24, 2009.

Preston, Rob. "Down to Business: Is Executive Pay Excessive?" *Information Week* (Informationweek.com), January 13, 2007.

Puzzanghera, Jim. "Attempts to Limit CEO Pay Have Yet to Succeed." *Los Angeles Times,* September 26, 2008.

———, Christi Parsons, and Walter Hamilton. "Wall Street Finds Ways Around Executive Pay Caps." *Los Angeles Times,* February 5, 2009.

Rauch, Jonathan. "Capitalism's Fault Lines." Book Review. *New York Times,* May 17, 2009.

Rector, Robert. "How Poor Are America's Poor?" The Heritage Foundation (Heritage.org), August 27, 2007.

Reich, Robert B. "CEO's Deserve Their Pay." *Wall Street Journal,* September 14, 2007.

Reitz, Allison. "Michael Jackson Memorial Tickets in Limited Supply, Draw High Asking Prices Online." Ticketnews.com, July 6, 2009.

Reutter, Mark. "Anti-Business Movies Reflect Makers' Dislike of Bosses Who Control Film." University of Illinois News Bureau, October 20, 2004.

Riedl, Brian M. "The Top 10 Examples of Government Waste." The Heritage Foundation, April 4, 2005.

Roberts, Joel. "Poll: Little Faith in Big Biz." CBS News (Cbsnews.com), July 10, 2002.

Roberts, Paul Craig. "The Seven Fat Years: And How to Do It Again." Book Review. *National Review,* September 14, 1992.

Roosevelt, Franklin D. Inaugural Speech. Washington, DC, March 4, 1933.

Roosevelt, Theodore. Acceptance Speech at the Progressive Party Convention. Chicago, August 6, 1912.

———. "Citizenship in a Republic." Paris, France, April 23, 1910.

———. State of the Union Message. Washington, DC, December 8, 1908.

Rosen, Christine. "This Boomer Isn't Going to Apologize." *Wall Street Journal,* June 19, 2009.

Rothbard, Murray N. "The Myth of Efficient Government Service." *Mises Daily,* March 18, 2004.

Rove, Karl. "Republicans and the Tea Parties." *Wall Street Journal,* April 16, 2009.

Saad, Lydia. "Nurses Shine, Bankers Slump in Ethics Ratings." Gallup.com, November 24, 2008.

Samuelson, Robert. "American Capitalism Besieged." *Washington Post,* March 24, 2009.

Schaefer, David. "Transit Plan Can Trace Surprise Success to Suburbs." *Seattle Times,* November 7, 1996.

Schrank, David and Tom Lomax. "Urban Mobility Report 2009." Texas Transportation Institute, July, 2009.

Schwartz, Nelson D. "As Spain's Economy Falters, Bank Holdups Are on the Rise." *New York Times,* July 21, 2009.

Sebastian, Eisla. "The Problems Facing the US National Park System." Associated Content (Associatedcontent.com), November 9, 2005.

Seidman, Gay. "A Humorous Perspective." Book Review. *The Harvard Crimson,* Online Edition, September 21, 2009.

Sengupta, Somini. "Crusader for India's Low Castes Sees Wealth as Cure." *New York Times,* August 30, 2008.

Seymour, Julia A. "New TNT Drama Pits 'Robin Hoods' Against 'Capitalist Victimizers.' " Business and Media Institute (Businessandmedia.org), December 12, 2008.

Shane, Scott A, "Should the Government Focus Resources on High-Potential Start-Ups?" *New York Times,* June 18, 2009.

Sherman, Stratford. "The Jack Welch Era: How Will History Remember Him?" HarperCollins (Harpercollins.com), accessed July 5, 2009.

Shorto, Russell. "Going Dutch." *New York Times Magazine,* May 3, 2009.

Slaughter, Matthew J. "What Is an 'American Car'?" *Wall Street Journal,* May 7, 2009.

Smith, Roy C. "Greed Is Good." *Wall Street Journal,* February 7, 2009.

Solomon, Deborah. "If He Builds It." *New York Times Magazine,* March 29, 2009.

Spors, Kelly K. "So You Want to Be an Entrepreneur." *Wall Street Journal,* February 23, 2009.

Stein, Alan J. "Turning Point 9: The Sound and the Ferry: The Birth of Washington State Ferries." Essay 3325, Historylink.org, June 1, 2001.

Stempel, Jonathan. "Grassley Backtracks on AIG Suicide Comments." Reuters, March 17, 2009.

Stevenson, Richard W. "Capitalism After the Fall." *New York Times,* April 19, 2009.

Stone, Oliver and Stanley Weiser. *Wall Street.* Twentieth Century Fox Film Corporation, 1987.

Strouse, Jean. "When the Economy Really Did 'Fall Off a Cliff.' " *New York Times,* March 23, 2009.

Sulkowicz, Kerry J., MD. "CEO Pay: The Prestige, The Peril." *Business Week,* November 20, 2006.

Swartz, Jon and Byron Acohido. "Without Jobs, Apple 'Will Survive But May Not Burn So Bright.' " *USA Today,* January 16, 2009.

Szasz, Thomas. "Universal Health Care Isn't Worth Our Freedom." *Wall Street Journal,* July 15, 2009.

"The Left's Collapse." Editorial. *Wall Street Journal,* June 20–21, 2009.

Thompson, Peter Wynn. "An Ad Hoc Strategy to Reverse the Decline in U.S. Factory Jobs." *New York Times,* July 21, 2009.

Tozzi, John. "The Entrepreneurship Myth." Book Review. *Business Week,* January 23, 2008.

"Travel Light: The Journey Begins 7/18/09." Official Brochure. Sound Transit, Seattle, WA, Summer 2009.

"Trends in Compliance Activities Through Fiscal Year 2009." Treasury Inspector General for Tax Administration, June 10, 2009.

Van Riper, Tom. "America's Most Admired Professions." *Forbes,* July 28, 2006.

VandeHei, Jim. "Candidate Decries Tax-Haven Firms While Accepting Executives Aid." *Washington Post,* February 26, 2004.

"Very Large Majorities of Americans Believe Big Companies, PACs, Political Lobbyists and the News Media Have Too Much Power and Influence in D.C." Harris Interactive (Harrisinteractive.com), March 12, 2009.

Wallison, Peter J. "How Geithner Can Price Troubled Bank Assets." *Wall Street Journal,* February 26, 2009.

"Washington State Ferries History/Creation of WSF." Washington State Department of Transportation (Wsdot.wa.gov), retrieved May 2007.

Wayne, Leslie. "Boeing Chief Is Ousted After Admitting Affair." *New York Times,* March 8, 2005.

Weisman, Jonathan. "Summer Calls Obama Defender of Free Markets." *Wall Street Journal,* June 13, 2009.

Welch, Jack. "It's Business Bashing Time." *Business Week,* March 10, 2008.

———. "Must Someone Lose?" *Business Week,* May 26, 2006.

———. "What About Non-Winners." *Business Week,* August 28, 2006.

Whiting, Richard A., Raymond B. Egan, and Gus Khan. "Ain't We Got Fun." Lyrics. 1921.

"Who Are the Highest Paid Players in Major League Baseball for 2009?" Associated Press, April 8, 2009.

Will, George F. "The 'Tax the Rich!' Reflex." *Newsweek,* July 27, 2009.

Yu, Roger. "Nearby Deals to the Rescue as National Park Visitation Slides." *USA Today,* July 16, 2009.

Zakaria, Fareed. Book Review. "'The World Is Flat': The Wealth of Yet More Nations." *New York Times,* May 1, 2005.

———. "Greed Is Good (To a Point)." *Newsweek,* June 22, 2009.

ACKNOWLEDGMENTS

In order to write this book, I had to steal time from an already crowded schedule. Those constraints left little chance to involve a broad array of friends and colleagues in the process of research and consultation, but those who did participate played serious roles.

Juggling my responsibilities successfully would have been impossible—in fact, unthinkable—without my longtime producer Jeremy Steiner ("Pride of Hillsdale College"), who's worked with me since the first week of my daily radio show more than thirteen years ago. It's no exaggeration to say that I'd never have begun this project, let alone finished it, without his enthusiastic support. Greg Tomlin ("Rock Star Greg"), my gifted associate producer on the radio, also participated in key decisions and confronted crucial challenges, particularly with the audiobook versions of both *The 10 Big Lies About America* and *The 5 Big Lies About American Business*.

Karmen Andersen Frisvold (yet another Hillsdale graduate!) worked first as an invaluable intern on the radio show and then took over from my previous "intrepid assistant" (Stacy Alderfer), who departed on maternity leave to care for her twin daughters. For more than a year, Karmen has been an unmitigated joy—reliable, dedicated, and gifted in finding precisely the re-search and resources I needed at any given moment.

Mary Choteborsky of Crown Forum/Random House took over as my editor just in time to guide *The 10 Big Lies About America* to bestseller status after its 2008 release and she has been a marvelously organized and insightful collaborator on this book from its inception. Her discipline and vision kept the work on track and steered me away from fatal distractions. Meanwhile, Jennifer Reyes, Mary's assistant, managed to tra-verse all obstacles in securing the visual images featured in these pages.

Finally, my wife, Dr. Diane Medved, contributed as always more than anyone else. She didn't write the bulk of the text (as she did with our coauthored project in 1997, *Saving Childhood*), nor did she prepare early drafts of many chapters (as she did with *The 10 Big Lies About America*). But she did advise and edit and proofread and inspire and research, spending dozens of nights with me till four in the morning (or occasionally till dawn) during the height of the writing process. We're coming up to our twenty-fifth anniversary, and there's something mon-umental about having shared absolutely everything for a quar-ter of a century. At the same time I feel proud, giddy, and perpetually surprised at the thought that we're on the same team, and the energy of that partnership still infuses every un-dertaking with a sense of joy and adventure.

Seattle

August 2009

INDEX